❧ beautiful windows

 beautiful
windows

*The Ultimate Window Treatment
Design Book*

Woman's Day, Special Interest Publications

First published in 2008 in the United States of America by
Filipacchi Publishing
1633 Broadway
New York, NY 10019

Woman's Day is a registered trademark of Hachette Filipacchi Media U.S., Inc.

EDITOR: Jennifer Ladonne
DESIGN: Patricia Fabricant
PRODUCTION: Ed Barredo

ISBN: 1-933231-40-8
Printed in China

CONTENTS

2295

FIRST CONSIDERATIONS

make your own

Even if you are a sewing novice, consider crafting your own window treatments. A DIY window project can be very easy to make and offers the following benefits:

- Save money—especially if you purchase the fabric on sale.

- Create the ideal window treatment for your decor; you're not limited to only what's available in catalogs or stores.

- Make a treatment the correct size and color; you don't have to settle for a less-than-perfect premade option.

- Select material you love and that matches your decor perfectly.

choosing a style

Selecting appropriate draperies is a little like putting together an outfit. They should enhance the bones of the room, support the way the room is used, and harmonize with your family's lifestyle. Keeping an idea file of looks you like can help you narrow your choices.

If your decor is casual, you may prefer an easy-to-open treatment that's also sturdy. Contemporary rooms can benefit from simple treatments that draw visual interest from texture rather than pattern or style. Traditional or formal rooms can handle more elaborate treatments, with several layers of panels or heavily draped fabrics and rich trims. Take into account the window's shape and whether you want to disguise or highlight certain features.

In addition to looking good, window treatments need to be functional. Is privacy a factor? Do you need to block the sun or highlight or downplay a view? Will the window treatment cover a door that opens to a seldom-used balcony or to the main outdoor entertaining space?

- If you live on a noisy street and need a sound barrier, consider incorporating a layered window treatment, such as full-length curtains over sheers with a valance as a topper.

- Create privacy from the outside world with a window treatment in an opaque material.

- Block an unattractive view while allowing in natural light with sheer fabrics.

- Increase curb appeal by lining window treatments that face the street with either white or off-white lining fabric for a finished look.

- Choose colored or patterned fabrics to add energy to the room, rather than playing it safe with neutral colors.

- Select a style that covers the entire opening of the window—such as a pull-down shade or floor-length curtain—to prevent bright, fabric-damaging sunlight from streaming into the room.

selecting fabrics

The style of your window treatment will influence your fabric choice. Along with color and print, consider texture, drapability and how the material will stand up to everyday use. Loose weaves can soften modern rooms, but may snag easily. Nubby fabrics add texture to modern and transitional settings; heavier fabrics, such as brocades and velvets, give a formal air. Synthetics and blends can be more durable, less expensive alternatives to fine silks and satins. Working through a designer will open an even wider assortment of options. Before you invest, bring home a sample to try at the window, observing how it drapes and how it looks in different lights.

Not all draperies need to be lined—the exception is silk, which must always be lined to protect it from sun damage—but a lining does give most treatments a more graceful drape. Stick to shades of white or ecru for linings to give windows a cohesive appearance from the street. Adding an interlining (also known as a bump) creates a heavier, more luxurious effect and provides another layer of insulation or light control. Do-it-yourselfers can line ready-mades to give them a more substantial look. Adding weights in the corners will also enhance their drape.

- Select the best-quality fabric you can afford; the finished project will last longer and look better.

- Consider using "seconds." Classified as a second simply because it is slightly off the manufacturer's standard, the fabric may be perfect for you.

- Look for fabrics specially made for decorating. They often have finishes applied to resist wrinkles, mildew, soiling and fading. These finishes can make the fabrics more expensive but are beneficial qualities.

- Be conscious that the color of a sheer fabric will appear more intense on the roll or bolt.

- Choose a solid-colored fabric with an element of texture for visual interest.

- Purchase a small amount of fabric and do a test run to see how it sews, presses and drapes before committing to many yards.

choosing hardware

Metal and wood are the basic choices in hardware. Matching finishes to existing woods and metals in the room guarantees a polished look. Traverse rods, once merely functional, are also appearing as decorative features, with brushed finishes in a range of metal tones.

For difficult-to-dress windows, such as curved or bay windows, swivel sockets allow rods to conform to the window's shape. If there's no stackback room (see *Measuring Basics*, page 14) for the drapery to clear the window, consider a swing-arm rod, which will clear the window when open. Use knobs to hang stationary panels from loops. Knobs also work well for draping valances around half-round windows. For privacy, hang rods above the top of the half-round window, so draperies can be closed at night.

Rods look best when hung above and beyond window edges. As a rule, if you can buy the hardware in a retail store you can install it yourself by following package directions. It does take patience and accurate measuring skills, however, so it may be wise to call in an installer. Be sure it's sturdy enough to hold your fabric, and choose the correct screws and anchors for your wall, be it drywall, wood or brick. Most rods hold 1½ pounds of fabric per linear foot; check out heavy-duty rods for weighty fabrics.

➤ Buy good-quality hardware from a reputable manufacturer. Don't try to save money by buying bargain brands—they usually aren't sturdy enough.

➤ Enlist a partner to help you install drapery hardware. Two sets of eyes are better than one when deciding on placement, and two sets of hands make installation easier.

➤ Allow for clearance between the layers if you'll be placing hardware over an existing treatment that will remain in place (such as adding a valance over floor-length curtains). The recommended distance is 2 inches. This guideline also applies when installing a fabric treatment over vertical or horizontal blinds.

➤ Since window treatments can be very heavy, mount hardware into a stud near the window. If you can't locate a stud, use wall anchors for additional support.

➤ Mount the brackets for the curtain rod 2 to 4 inches above the top edge of the window frame and 2 to 4 inches out from each side of the window frame. Avoid placing the brackets on the window frame if at all possible, as the frame may split.

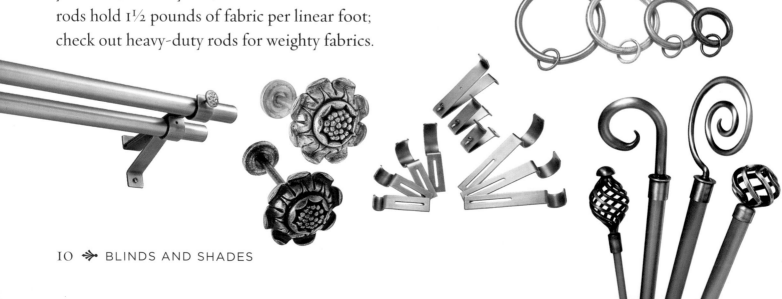

choosing and hanging the right window treatment

Even the most elegant room falls short if the window treatment isn't just right. Like wall color, draperies can help pull a room together or create a backdrop for the room's furnishings. They can accentuate a window's shape, disguise its faults, frame a view or conceal it—and there's no end to the variety of looks and styles. Whether you choose to invest in custom panels, go for ready-made or even make your own, keep these tips in mind as you sort through the options.

pros and cons

When it comes to purchasing curtains, there are several choices: ready-made, semi-custom, or custom. The type you opt for depends on your budget and the difficulty of the drapery project. Here's what you should consider:

ready-made
- Ready to hang
- Easy on the budget
- Offered in coordinated collections
- Limited selection of patterns, colors and sizes

semi-custom
- Wide selection of fabrics and patterns
- Less expensive than custom
- Accommodates unusual sizes
- Limited to styles offered
- Require careful measurement

custom draperies
- Virtually limitless selection of fabrics and styles
- Measurements, ordering and installation by a pro
- Most expensive option

the perfect heading

Combined with fabric, the heading, or top, of a drapery is key in defining its overall style. For a contemporary treatment, consider simple grommets that slip through the rod. If space is tight, panels with grommets require less room when they are open. Rings at the tops of panels can achieve a similar look as well as add several inches of length to ready-made panels. To give draperies a fuller appearance, consider one of several styles of pleats. Elegant goblet pleats work in traditional settings, inverted pleats create a no-fuss heading suitable for modern rooms, and classic pinch pleats adapt to any decor. For a sumptuous and feminine look, try a shirred or gathered heading.

For a more formal look, consider covering the tops of draperies with swags and jabots in traditional rooms. Plain or box-pleated fabric valances or wood cornices provide a clean way to add polish to contemporary curtains. To keep valances in correct proportion, make sure their height equals 20 percent of the total length of the treatment.

ABOVE: Classic finials, brackets and holdbacks are ideal for traditional-style curtains. Choose a style that suits your decor.

As you consider headings, think about how often you'll open and close the draperies. Pleated panels installed on traverse rods will always have a uniform look at the top, while panels that must be opened by hand will have to be arranged every time you move them. Gathered panels installed on rods are difficult to open and close, but the look can be imitated with shirring tape so panels can be installed with hooks on a traverse rod. For do-it-yourselfers, fabric stores carry header tapes that take the tediousness out of placing pleats by hand. Options include those for making shirred tops as well as for several styles of pleats.

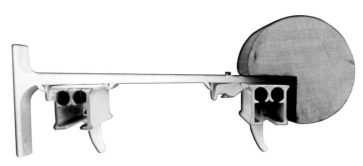

ABOVE: A double traverse rod allows layered draperies—such as a panel and a sheer—to be drawn open and closed smoothly on a track, while concealing the underlying hardware.

put together a window treatment that suits your style

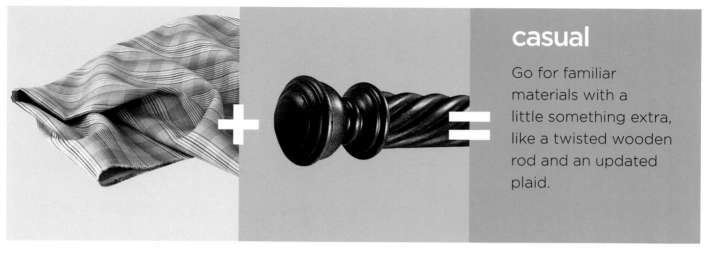

casual

Go for familiar materials with a little something extra, like a twisted wooden rod and an updated plaid.

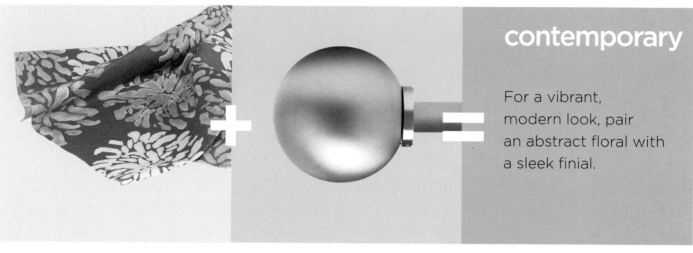

contemporary

For a vibrant, modern look, pair an abstract floral with a sleek finial.

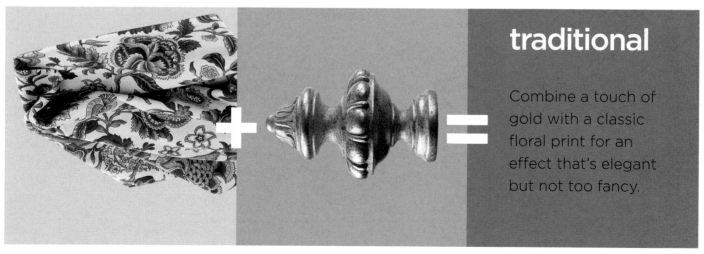

traditional

Combine a touch of gold with a classic floral print for an effect that's elegant but not too fancy.

measuring basics

Before starting your panel or shade project, decide how and where you will mount it in order to determine its finished length. You can mount valances and pelmets either outside or inside. Cornices should be mounted on the outside of a window frame.

Consider these factors to help you achieve the look you desire:

↠ inside mount: Shades mounted inside a frame should have a finished length 1/4 inch shorter than the height of the window from top to bottom inside the frame. Measure the width of the window opening: the recess should be at least 3½ inches deep in order to accommodate a mounting board or other mounting hardware.

↠ outside mount: Measure inside the frame at the top and at the bottom of the window; a window can be narrower at one end.

For an outside-mounted treatment, make sure it's at least 2 inches wider than any window treatment it may be layered over and deep enough to fit comfortably over any hardware. The depth, which is called the return, can be from 4½ to 7 inches.

Measure the width to be covered and add 3½ inches for a standard valance return. If layered over another treatment, add at least 5½ inches for the return. The length of the topper should be in proportion to the window or treatment—or equal to one-fifth of the overall length.

Shades mounted outside the frame should be positioned on mounting boards either near the crown molding or ceiling or halfway between the top of the window frame and the base of the crown molding or ceiling. Finished shade length for such shades should equal the distance from the top of the mounting board to the sill or to the bottom of the molding below the sill.

↠ rod height: The finished length of panels should be measured from the top or bottom of the mounted rod, depending on the header type and/or rings you'll use. Rods should ideally be positioned just beneath the crown molding at the ceiling or halfway between the top of the window frame and the ceiling.

↠ sill length: The finished length of short panels should end 1/4 inch above the sill or at the bottom of the molding below the sill.

↠ floor length: Finished panels should end about 1/2 inch above the floor.

↠ break length: Measure from the top or bottom of the rod and add 1 to 2 inches to get the finished length of floor-length panels that gracefully sweep the floor.

For a tailored-looking valance, multiply the window frame width by 1½ to get your overall fabric width. For a gathered valance, cut a rectangle that is two and a half to three times the actual width of the window.

Kitchen window valances can be shorter in length, but most valances measure between 15 and 20 inches in length, depending on the window. A good rule of thumb: Your finished valance should be one-fifth the length of the overall treatment or window height.

Create a gathered look by stitching on a casing along the top of your window treatment. The hemmed casing should be about two times the diameter of your rod.

measuring tips

➤ Mount the hardware before taking any measurements. More accurate measurements can be taken if the hardware is in place.

➤ Use a stepladder to reach the top of the window when taking measurements and use a retractable steel tape measure, not cloth or plastic, which can stretch. Unlike cloth tape, it won't sag and will therefore give you perfect results.

➤ Have someone else hold one end of the tape measure in position when you're taking measurements.

➤ Measure each window in the same room and record its location. They may all look the same size, but often they are not.

➤ Measure for the finished length of floor-length curtains in several places across the width of the window. Floors can be uneven and windows may be out of plumb, so use the shortest measurement as the finished length or the curtain will buckle on the bottom edge. If the floor is carpeted, lay a piece of cardboard over the carpet to get more accurate measurements.

➤ Check all measurements twice before purchasing fabric, paper, wood or other supplies.

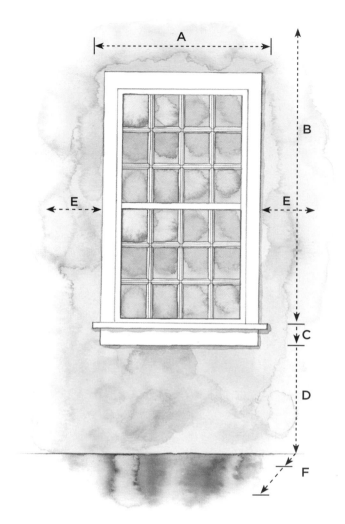

Accurate measurements are crucial. Measure twice, just to be sure, and use a steel tape. Ideally, the horizontal measurement of your rod should be approximately 6 to 20 inches wider than the window frame, depending on wall space (**A**). For length, take one of three measurements from the top of the mounted rod (which ideally should be just below crown molding or halfway between crown molding and top of frame): to the top of the sill (**B**), to the bottom of the apron (**C**) or to the floor (**D**).

• The width of each panel should be 1½ to 2½ times that of the window. For sheer fabrics, the ratio is three to one. For lining and interlining, order the same amount of fabric.

• Allow for stackback, the amount of wall space needed to accommodate a fully opened drapery (**E**). It should be about one-sixth of the frame's width on each side.

• Most designers recommend a 1- to 2-inch break at the floor. If panels will be opened and closed daily, ¼ to ½ inch of clearance at the floor will permit them to operate smoothly.

• For a particularly elegant effect, stationary panels can be puddled, so extra fabric is gracefully arranged on the floor. Common allowances are 6 inches and 9 inches (**F**).

define your type of window

Guide to six of the most popular decorative styles.

CIRCLE TOP
Shaped like a half circle, this window can be used alone or above another window. Above a door, a circle-top window lets light stream without giving outsiders a look in. These windows are usually fixed.

CLERESTORY
The term "clerestory" originally referred to the upper reaches of a cathedral. Clerestory windows, usually fixed, can be used singly or in a row near the top of a wall, often in a great room or landing.

PICTURE
Picture windows are extra-large, usually wider than they are tall. Their size can overwhelm a smaller room, but they are well suited to big family rooms or master bedrooms.

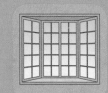

BAY AND BOW
In a bay window, three or more windows are set at angles of 30 to 45 degrees. A bow window has three or more windows fixed at a wider angle, around 10 degrees, to create a softer circle.

CUSTOM
As the name implies, custom windows are cut to order in almost any shape. They complement a home's unique look and serve as a focal point. Usually fixed, they can be conversation starters in any room.

PALLADIAN
Also called Venetian windows, a central window, usually arched, is flanked by two smaller windows. They have a formal look that's meant to be seen, so they usually adorn the front of a house.

energy-saving blackout drapes

In neutral tones that complement any decor, these curtains will look luxurious in your home while saving you money. They're made from soft microsuede polyester and are backed with an acrylic foam, enabling temperature regulation by sometimes drafty windows, keeping rooms warm in winter and cool in summer. The pairs of 100-inch-wide panels come in four different lengths to fit your windows like custom draperies. With a room-darkening capability, they are perfect for sleepers who are sensitive to light, or night-shift workers who need to sleep during the day. Furthermore, they could not be easier to maintain: simply machine-wash cold then line-dry, no ironing needed!

a guide to the tools of the stitchless trade

ITEM	DESCRIPTION	PROS & CONS
	DOUBLE-SIDED FABRIC TAPE and **GLUE DOTS** are dry adhesives that instantly bond without ironing. Best for trim, ribbon, beading and appliqués, fabric tape comes in common ribbon widths and glue dots vary in circumference and thickness.	**PROS:** No-mess portion control and precise application in a single step. **CONS:** Because it is extremely strong and already dry, a mistake could be permanent. **COST:** low (sold as package).
	FUSIBLE WEB is an adhesive-soaked material that is activated with the heat of an iron to join fabrics together. It comes in rolls that allow you to join lengthy panels, sheets that can be cut to size, and precut strips that can be used with ribbon and trim. Simply position a piece between the two surfaces you want to adhere and iron it to fuse.	**PROS:** The webbing comes in different strengths, so you can select one that will work for your specific project. **CONS:** Repeated washing might cause the edges of the joined fabric to separate over time. **COST:** low for precut piece; medium to high for 25- to 75-yard rolls.
	A **GROMMET** is a metal ring used to secure a hem and reinforce a hole in curtain fabric for curtain rings or laces. Smaller grommets can be snapped or hammered into place, but larger grommets will require a special tool—and a little more muscle—to press them through the fabric.	**PROS:** Grommets can support the weight of a full-length curtain and stand up to pulling. **CONS:** Large grommets require hefty (and relatively pricey) tools. **COST:** low for small grommets to medium for large grommets; setting tools, low to medium.
	HOOK-AND-LOOP MATERIAL can be used to close seams or attach a decorative fabric element, such as a valance, directly to a surface. It usually comes in strips, with iron-on glue backing to adhere it to fabrics, or dry adhesive backing to adhere it to flat surfaces—like a wall or bed frame. Use it on seams that you plan to reopen or to apply seasonal embellishments.	**PROS:** The glue backing actually gets stronger when you wash it. **CONS:** Hook-and-loop tape is relatively thick, so a seam may appear slightly raised. **COST:** low for 12 1-inch strips; medium for 15 feet of tape.
	FABRIC GLUE can be used to join fabrics or appliqués and to make hems and seams. Apply as you would a normal glue, using a brush or your fingertip to create a smooth, even coating. This glue is tacky until is has bonded, and then it dries either on its own or with an iron. Most brands provide a bond that lasts through washing and dry cleaning.	**PROS:** The glue isn't permanent until it has dried, so you can adjust the placement or rinse it away with water. **CONS:** Be sure to test the glue on scrap fabric. It might not be strong enough for a heavy material, like leather, and could bleed through a sheer fabric. **COST:** low for 1.25 ounces.

2

BLINDS
AND
SHADES

DRAPED

⚜ billowy draped shades

SKILL LEVEL: beginner

curtain rod and mounting hardware
screwdriver
steel tape measure
lightweight sheer fabric
chalk marking pencil
pins
iron
scissors
matching thread
sewing machine
matching scalloped trim
½-inch white plastic rings
hand sewing needle
awl
small metal screw-in eyelets
shade cord
cord pull
cleat and mounting hardware

1. Mount curtain rod at desired distance above window.

2. Measure desired length of shade (from rod to sill); add 7 inches. Measure window width; double this measurement. Mark and cut one fabric panel to these measurements for each window.

3. Turn under ½ inch, then 1 inch, on each long edge of each panel; pin and press. Stitch close to folds to hem side edges.

4. Turn under ½ inch, then 3 inches, on upper and lower edge of each panel; pin and press. Stitch close to folds to hem lower edge and form rod pocket on top.

5. Pin trim under lower edge of each panel, turning under 1 inch on ends. Stitch close to panel edge.

6. Mark ring placement on wrong side of shade as follows: Mark a line across shade about 10 inches from lower edge, then mark additional lines above this one, spacing remaining lines about 14 inches apart and ending at stitching line on upper hem. Mark ring placement along these lines, placing a ring near each side edge and spacing remaining rings evenly about 20 inches apart along each line.

7. Hand sew a ring at each mark.

8. Mark placement of eyelets on underside of window frame, spacing eyelets same as ring spacing. Use awl to make guide holes at marks, then screw in eyelets.

9. Double window height and add width; cut a piece of cord for each vertical row of rings to this measurement.

10. Tie a cord to each lower ring, then thread cords upward through each vertical row.

11. Hang shade on rod. Thread each cord through eyelet directly above it.

12. Determine which side of shade cord will hang on. Thread each cord through remaining eyelets across top so all cords hang on desired side.

13. Slip cords through pull; knot ends together about halfway down window and trim excess.

14. Mount cleat on wall just above cord ends; wrap cord around cleat to hold shade at desired height.

challenge: Enjoy the view but have privacy. The window seat in the corner of this dining room lets one sit and enjoy the view. What type of treatment would work here but also provide privacy when needed?

solution: Opulent Roman shades. Shades hug the wall more closely than draperies, a consideration in a tight space where seating meets windows. The shades shown here are made of a lightweight silken fabric to match the wall color, softening the corner without adding busyness. When raised, the shades create the look of an elegant valance that draws the eye up and calls attention to the windows' height. For privacy, shades can be lowered to pillow-height, so they will not interfere with seat cushions. If privacy is not an issue, a simple valance can substitute for a shade.

challenge: The arched bay window and window seat are lovely in this girl's room, but curtains are a problem.

solution: Flatter the window's natural shape with graceful swags and jabots hung from an arched rod. Pull the window seat into the decor with matching billowy side panels and blend-in blinds.

challenge: This bay window is long and extra wide. How can it seem warmer and more inviting?

solution: An expanse of windows can be cold, so connect and cozy them up with a span of balloon shades that beckon sunlight and soften the glass. A cushioned window seat urges occupants to rest and gaze out.

❧ striped roll-up shade

A blue-and-white color scheme is a kitchen classic, and it works well with many accent colors.
This roll-up shade adjusts to any height, and the ties can be made of colorful ribbon instead of matching fabric.

SKILL LEVEL: beginner

yardstick

chalk marking pencil

scissors

cotton fabric

pins

matching thread

sewing machine

iron

heavy-duty stapler

½ x 1-inch wood board, cut to inside window width

screws

drill and drill driver

1. Measure length and width of inside of window frame; add 1 inch to width and 1½ inches to length. Mark and cut two pieces of fabric to these measurements for shade. Cut two 5-inch-wide pieces of fabric by double the length measurement for ties, piecing fabric as needed (be sure to match stripes if piecing fabric).

2. Pin shade sections together, with right sides facing and raw edges even. Stitch side and bottom edges with 2½-inch seams. Trim seams and clip corners; turn right side out. Press. Zigzag stitch top edge closed.

3. Fold each tie in half lengthwise, with right sides facing and raw edges even. Stitch edges with ½-inch seams, leaving 10-inch opening along long edge. Trim seams and clip corners; turn right side out. Press. Slip-stitch opening closed.

4. Drape centers of ties over upper edge of shade, placing ties about 6 to 8 inches from each end of shade. Topstitch through upper edge of shade and both layers of ties, so two ends hang in front of shade and two ends hang in back.

5. Staple upper edge of shade to board. Drill starter holes through board, then mount board with screws to inside of window frame.

⊰ country roll-up shade

SKILL LEVEL: beginner

two tones of fabric equal to the length of the window plus 6″

yardstick

marking pencil chalk

scissors

hand sewing needle

matching thread

Fray-Check glue (optional)

iron

sewing machine with buttonhole attachment

pins

two or more buttons no more than ³⁄₄″ in diameter

4 yards of 1½″-wide ribbon, cut into two 55″-long pieces and two 12″-long pieces

one piece of 1″ x 2″ wood, cut to inside width of window minus ½″

staple gun

drill with ⅛″ bit and screwdriver bit

three to five #6, 2¼″ flathead screws

plastic wall anchors (optional)

Note: This shade was designed to be inside-mounted.

1. Measure, mark and cut one piece of fabric equal to half the desired width of shade plus 1 inch for seam allowances, and two pieces of contrasting fabric equal to one fourth the width of the shade plus 1½ inches for seam allowances and side hems. Zig-zag stitch or apply Fray-Check glue to all raw edges.

2. Iron all pieces, and pin one side edge of both side pieces to sides of center piece with right sides facing.

Sew all three pieces together with ½ inch seams. Fold both seams toward center panel and press. Fold and press a ½ inch double hem along bottom and side edges and topstitch to hem.

3. On backside, along the two seams, measure and mark the placement of your buttons. (Note: Approximately 5 inches of the top of the shade will wrap around the mounting board, so the top of the face of your finished shade will start about 5 inches from the top of the unfinished shade. The buttons should be approximately 13 inches to 25 inches from the top edge of the shade, depending on where you want your shade to gather.) Machine or hand sew buttons to the back of the shade at each mark. (Note: Several sets of buttons can be sewn onto the back to create different lengths.)

4. Machine sew buttonholes near one end of each 12 inch-long ribbon. On the front side of shade sew the opposite short edge of each 12 inch-long ribbon directly over the seam just above the buttons sewn onto the backside. Gather the bottom edge up toward both buttons and draw the ribbons around the gathered fabric, and slip buttonholes over buttons to secure gathered edge in place. Tie two floppy bows from the 55 inch-long ribbons and hand stitch the ribbons on top of the stitched short end of each 12 inch-long ribbon to disguise raw edges.

5. Starting at the top front edge of the mounting board, wrap the top edge of the shade under the board and over the top so that the top edge of the shade hangs from the front top edge of the board. Using the staple gun, staple the fabric to the top of the board.

6. Using the ⅛ inch drill bit, predrill two holes through the underside of the 2 inch-wide board approximately 3 inches in from each end of wood. Predrill another hole in the center and predrill additional holes if necessary, depending on the width of your window. Drive in the screws through the holes to secure the shade in place, using plastic wall anchors if necessary.

london shade

SKILL LEVEL: beginner

4 x 1-inch wood board, cut to ½ inch less than inside window width

yardstick

fabric: decorator fabric, contrasting decorator fabric and lining

scissors

chalk marking pencil

pins

sewing machine

matching thread

hand-sewing needle

plastic rings

iron

monofilament thread

cleat and mounting hardware

awl

small screw eyes

heavy-duty staple gun

about 8 yards of shade cord

drill and drill driver or screwdriver

1. Measure length of mounting board; add 5 inches for fabric width. Measure desired length of shade from upper to lower edge of window; add 4 inches for fabric length. Cut print fabric to these measurements.

2. For inner pleats, cut two pieces of checked fabric, each 12 inches wide and same length as print fabric. For lining, add 22 inches to print fabric width; cut lining to this width and same length as other fabric.

3. Measure and mark lines vertically along print fabric, about 12 inches from each end; cut along lines to form two side panels and one center panel.

4. Pin checked panels to corresponding edges of center panel, with right sides facing and raw edges even; stitch with ½-inch seams. Pin and stitch a side panel to each checked panel in same manner to complete front of shade. Press seams open.

5. Trim 1 inch from each side edge and lower edge of lining. Place shade wrong side up; place lining wrong side down on shade, centering it vertically and aligning the upper edges. Pin all edges of lining to shade.

6. Turn under ½ inch, then 1¼ inches, on side edges of shade, covering edges of lining; press. Hem edges with hand blind stitch.

7. To form each pleat, draw the seams on both sides of contrasting panel together, folding the fabric so right sides of fabric are facing inside the pleat and centering contrasting fabric between seams along length. Pin and stitch from upper and lower edges 2 inches along the seam where front fabric meets to hold pleats in place. Press pleats open so they are centered behind stitched ends.

8. Turn under 1 inch, then 1 inch again, on lower edge of shade, covering edges of lining; press. Stitch close to fold hem shade. Baste top edge of pleats in place.

9. Mark line down center of each pleat on lining side of shade. Starting 1 inch from bottom, mark ring placement, spacing rings about 6 to 8 inches apart, stopping 2 inches from top.

10. Using monofilament thread, hand stitch a ring at each mark, being careful not to catch folded edges of pleats in stitching.

11. Finish upper raw edge of shade with a narrow zigzag or overcast stitch.

12. Attach cleat to side of window where you wish cords to hang.

13. Wrap and staple lining fabric around mounting board. Using awl, measure and mark placement of screw eyes on lower edge board, spacing eyes same distance apart as center of pleats.

14. Staple shade to upper edge of board.

15. Cut cord in half; tie one end of each cord to lowest ring in each row. Thread each cord up through all rings in each row, then up through screw eye directly above rings.

16. Thread cord from side opposite cleat through remaining screw eye, so both cords hang on cleat side. Cut ends even with lower edge of shade. Draw cord ends through cord pull; knot cords.

17. Drill starter holes through mounting board and screw board into upper inside edge of window.

⚜ roll-up shade

Brighten up a window-seat area with colorful fabrics and an easy roll-up shade.

NO SEW

SKILL LEVEL: beginner

fabric

steel tape measure

scissors

fusible adhesive

wood slat to fit width of shade

iron

Velcro brand Fabric Fusion tape (no-sew)

curtain rods: standard; 2½-inch wide, flat; 2½-inch wide, flat tension

fabric flowers

grosgrain ribbon

1. Cut fabric panel to fit window height plus 8 inches and window width plus 6 inches. At top and bottom turn in 1 inch. Form 1½-inch double side hems; using fusible adhesive, fuse in place. Turn lower edge up 3 inches; fuse hem in place.
2. Slip slat into bottom hem to stiffen.
3. Iron on loop section of Fabric Fusion tape to wrong side of shade, lining up strips with vertical mullions or as desired; iron on two strips of loop of Fabric Fusion

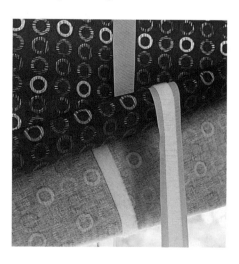

tape along wrong side of top edge.
4. Cut ribbons 1 foot longer than shade; iron on hook portion of Fabric Fusion tape to wrong side and across upper edge and lower third of ribbon.
5. Attach top edge of ribbon to loop of Fabric Fusion tape across top of

shade so ribbon will flip to front.
6. Join hook and loop of Fabric Fusion tapes and flip valance over top edge of rod to the front. Install rod with front side of rod next to window.
7. Roll up shade and adjust ribbon slings at back (see detail, left).

ROMAN

gingham roman shade

SKILL LEVEL: beginner

- steel tape measure
- metal ruler
- chalk marking pencil
- decorator fabric
- scissors
- lining
- pins
- hand-sewing needle
- matching thread
- iron
- sewing machine with zipper foot
- ring tape
- piping cord
- 1 x 2 mounting board cut to fit finished shade
- stapler
- 2-inch wood screws
- cord pull
- drill driver
- thin cord
- shade cleat

1. Measure inside width and height of window frame. Measure, mark and cut fabric 4 inches wider by 1 inch longer than desired finished shade. Cut lining to finished shade width by 1 inch longer than finished shade length. For valance, cut fabric equal to width of unfinished shade by 1/5 of finished shade length plus 3 inches. Cut lining to finished shade width by 1/5 of finished shade length plus 3 inches.

2. Center lining over decorator fabric, wrong sides together on a flat surface, pin and baste at top and bottom to secure. Repeat for valance.

3. Turn under and press a 1-inch double-fold hem along side edges of shade and blind hemstitch in place, stopping short 1 inch from bottom hem and leaving bottom hem open. Repeat for valance.

4. On shade lining, mark two vertical lines, evenly spaced apart at about 9 inches in from the side edges of the shade. (For windows 36 inches wide or less, you will only need to draw one vertical line down the center of the lining.)

5. Cut ring tape to fit, pin in place along side hems and marked lines, making sure rings line up horizontally. Sew tape to lining fabric only.

6. To make scalloped edge, divide bottom edge into sixths and draw six even scallops on lining side. Repeat for valance. Cut scalloped edges.

7. Cut two strips of piping cord, each long enough to cover scalloped edges. From decorator fabric, cut several 2-inch-wide bias strips of fabric. Square off short ends of strips and sew together with 1/2-inch seams to form one continuous casing, long enough to cover the piping cord. Wrap casing over piping cord, right side out raw edges matching, and stitch as close to cord as possible using a zipper foot.

8. Turn shade inside out, right sides facing. Sandwich piping between lining and face fabric along scalloped edge, raw edges matching; pin in place. Cut piping cord at both finished side hems, opening casing and leaving 1 inch of fabric to extend past each end. Repeat for valance.

9. Stitch through lining, piping and face fabric, as close to cord as possible. Turn shade right side out, and hand tack side hem in place, folding under excess fabric as needed for neat side edges. Press. Repeat for valance.

10. On a surface, place valance on top of shade, right sides up, raw edges together, and pin in place. Sew valance and shade together with 1/2-inch seam. Finish raw edge with a zigzag stitch, clipping excess. Press shade and valance.

11. Position shade and valance over mounting board, aligning seam with back edge of board and staple in place. Install screw eyes into underside of board, aligning them with each row of rings.

12. Place shade face down on a flat surface. Decide whether draw cord will hang on right or left side of shade. Tie thin cord on bottom ring of row on opposite side of draw. Thread cord through all rings of row and screw eye, then across through all screw eyes, extending cord about three-fourths the way down the draw side of shade. Repeat for remaining rows, threading through remaining top screw eyes until complete. Thread cords through pull and knot together. Tie on cord pull.

13. Using 2- or 3-inch wood screws, attach mounting board to top of window frame. Screw cleat to side of frame where desired.

challenge: Dealing with transoms. Transoms over a corner wall of windows add light to this casual dining room, but at times the sun's glare is just too strong; plus the owners coveted privacy.

solution: Fabric shades mounted inside the window frame display the full effect of the transom while providing light control and privacy. The smart gold-tone cotton stripe coordinates with the mellow yellow walls and the pretty floral pattern of the chair cushions.

❧ damask shade

An unfussy shade-on-shade ensemble is a space-saving choice for a compact neoclassical bedroom. This celery damask shade was trimmed with silk tassels. Underneath, a translucent roller shade of natural materials makes a stay-put backdrop for casual accents that "weight" the treatment and lead the eye upward.

SKILL LEVEL: intermediate

steel tape measure
chalk marking pencil
medium-weight damask fabric
scissors
pins
lining fabric
sewing machine
iron
curtain ring tape
½-inch-wide fusible hem tape
hand sewing needle
matching thread
2-inch-long beaded trim
self-adhesive hook-and-loop tape
1 x 1-inch wood, cut ½ inch shorter
    than inner width of window
3 screw eyes
shade cord or thin cotton cord
drill
2-inch screws
cord pull
cleat and screws

1. Measure inside width of window; add ½ inch. Measure inside length of window; add 4 inches. Cut fabric and lining to these measurements.
2. Pin fabric to lining, with right sides facing and raw edges even. Sew sides and lower edge with ½-inch seams. Trim corners; turn right side out. Press. Turn upper raw edges in ½ inch; press and topstitch closed.
3. Turn lower edge up 2 inches; press. Cut three pieces of ring tape, each as long as finished shade, making sure 2 inches of tape extend below the first ring on each piece. Cut three pieces of fusible hem tape to this length.
4. Measure and mark ring tape placement as follows: Mark a line along the length of the shade about 1 inch from each long edge and down center. Center fusible hem tape, then ring tape, over each line, positioning bottom rings 1 inch above the top of the hemline, sandwiching tape under the pressed hem. Rings should align on all three pieces. Fuse in place.
5. For extra strength, handstitch top of each ring through lining and face fabric.
6. Hand stitch or machine hemstitch lower hem in place. Handstitch beaded trim to bottom edge of shade, turning ends under ½ inch.
7. Cut hook-and-loop tape to shade width. Separate sections; attach loop section to lining side of upper edge of shade. Attach hook section to one long edge of wood.
8. Attach screw eyes to opposite long edge of wood, spacing them in alignment with rings on shade.
9. Cut three pieces of cord, each twice as long as window length. Tie a cord to bottom ring in one row, then slip cord up through each ring in sequence. Tie and thread cord through each row of rings in same manner.
10. Press hook-and-loop tape sections together to attach shade to wood with screw eyes facing down. Slip each cord through screw eye directly above it.
11. Determine which side of window you wish cords to hang. Slip opposite and center cord through other rings across top so all cords hang on this side.
12. Drill four holes, evenly spaced, through wood piece and top of shade between screw eyes, and screw wood to top of window frame.
13. Slip cord ends through pull; knot about halfway down window. Trim excess cord.
14. Screw cleat to wall about halfway down window. Pull cords to raise shade to desired height; wrap around cleat.

challenge: The grand proportions of this gracious and formal living room posed a hazard: Surrounded by a high ceiling and soaring windows, the window seat could easily have been overwhelmed. Draperies were called for to help define the window seat and lend it a personal scale. Accessories were needed to give it a warm, inviting appearance.

solution: Though the seat itself is large and the architectural details around it are sophisticated and strong, a sunny, casual mood pervades this welcoming nook. Bordered printed panels can be drawn to create privacy for someone perched on the seat, while crisp shades over the high transoms control light from above. The subdued yet cheerful color scheme completes the sunny picture.

roman shade with self-pelmet

SKILL LEVEL: intermediate

yardstick

level

chalk marking pencil

4 x ¾-inch mounting board, cut
  to a length 2 inches wider than
  window frame level

scissors

decorator fabric

lining

pins

matching thread

 sewing machine

rings

iron

staple gun

cord

drill with screw bits

wood crews

cleat

two or three L-shaped mounting
  brackets and mounting hardware,
  including mollys or wall anchors,
  if necessary

cleat and mounting hardware

1. Using a level and yardstick, measure and mark the desired placement of the valance across the window. Hold the board in place at these marks; mark the placement of the brackets outside of the window frame and on the underside of the board.

2. Determine dimensions of valance by dividing finished length measurement of shade by five and adding 2½ inches for the height, and measuring the length of the mounting board plus twice the length of return plus 1 inch for the width. Measure, mark and cut the fabric and lining to these dimensions.

3. Determine dimensions of shade by measuring length of mounting board plus 1 inch for width, and measuring from the finished height of the shade to the window sill plus 3¾ inches for length. Measure, mark and cut lining and fabric to these dimensions.

4. Place lining and fabric of both pelmet and shade together, right sides up, and pin. Stitch along the two side edges and the bottom edge of the pelmet with a ½-inch seam allowance. Stitch along the two side edges of the shade with a ½-inch seam allowance. Turn both pieces right side out and press.

5. Turn under bottom edge of shade ½ inch and press, turn under again ¾ inch and press, hemstitch in place. Center pelmet over shade, right sides up, and zigzag stitch the two pieces together along raw top edge.

6. Mark two vertical lines 8 inches in from each side edge on the lining side of the shade. Mark additional vertical lines, evenly spaced, about 12 inches from the first two lines along the shade. Beginning about 5 inches from the top of the casing along the bottom edge, mark positions for the rings every 7 to 8 inches along center of each side edge and along each line, stopping about 10 inches from the top edge. Stitch rings in place at each mark.

7. Fold back top of pelmet and shade 2 inches and press. Align folded edge of wrong side of shade with top edge of mounting board; staple in place, folding pelmet ends around the returns.

8. Mark placement of screw eyes on underside of board, directly above each vertical row of rings. Use drill to make small pilot holes; screw eyes in place.

9. Cut a piece of cord for each vertical row, each 2½ times the length of window. Tie a cord to bottom ring on each vertical row. String cord up through each ring in each row, then through screw eye above. Decide whether cords will hang on left or right side of window, then string cord or cords through screw eye or eyes toward the one on cord side, so all cords go through this screw eye and hang on one side of shade.

10. Using a drill, attach the L brackets to mounting board with wood screws. Insert mollys or wall anchors in the drill holes, if necessary, and mount the shade. With the shade lowered, adjust cord length so tension is equal on all cords, thread the cords through the pull, then knot the cords together about three quarters of the way down shade. Trim excess cord below knot.

11. Screw cleat to wall about halfway down window length; pull cords to raise shade to desired level, then wrap them around cleat to secure shade.

challenge: This guest room has lots of windows, including a bay where the bed doubles as a sofa. How provide privacy without interfering with the views?

solution: Try stitched-tuck shades, as simple and direct in style as your room's furnishings. Narrow top-stitched tucks give these Roman shades a very tailored look, adding a strong horizontal to the room. The background color of the shades should blend with the wall color, and any pattern should be subtle and unobtrusive. Here, the faint leaf pattern complements both the view and the room's natural elements. Give top edges a finished look with plain, narrow valances.

⊰ simple slatted shade

Create a simple slatted shade by cutting balsa-wood slats to fit, painting them and linking together with beads and embroidery thread to mimic the look of high-end custom blinds.

SKILL LEVEL: beginner

steel tape measure

metal ruler

pencil

2-inch-wide wood slats, cut to fit within window frame (we used ³/₃₂-inch-thick pieces of balsa wood)

saw or craft knife

½-inch diameter wooden dowel, cut to fit within window frame

paint brushes

primer

latex paint

6-ply embroidery matching thread or thin string or cord

wood or other large-holed beads (³/₈ to ½ inch in diameter)

two ½-inch screw hooks

1. Measure the inside width and length of your window frame. Determine how many slats you'll need by dividing the length of the window frame by 2½ minus 2 inches. Measure, mark and cut wood slats (if using balsa-wood slats, cut with craft knife) and dowel to width measurement minus ¼ inch.

2. Brush slats and dowel with primer on one side, let dry. Turn over and prime other sides, let dry. Then repeat this process with latex paint—applying two coats if necessary and letting dry between coats.

3. Cut two pieces of embroidery thread, string or cord equal in length to twice the inside length of

window frame plus 8 inches. Fold one piece of string in half over the dowel about two inches from one end and thread the ends through two beads. Open the ends of string, insert a slat between the open strings, close the strings and thread through another bead. Repeat this process until all slats and beads are attached. After threading on last bead, knot the string two or three times to secure and cut off excess string or thread. Repeat this process on other side of dowel.

4. If desired, paint screw hooks to match shade, let dry. Insert screw hooks to top of window frame about 2 inches in from either side; finish with hooks facing forward. Place dowel onto hooks to hang shade. To lift shade, pull bottom beads up and hang on hooks.

challenge: Placed directly in the path of the setting sun, this cozy window seat called for smartly designed window treatments that would cut the glare and make the space inviting for somebody planning to spend the afternoon napping or reading. Since the seat is in a bedroom, they also had to provide privacy and access to views when desired.

solution: Venetian blinds allow the homeowner to control exactly how much light she wants to stream into the room at a given time. By tilting the blinds slightly, it's possible to filter the light without blocking it out entirely. A pretty ruffled valance up above ties into the color scheme of the room and complements the pillows on the seat.

⊸ slatted bathroom shade

SKILL LEVEL: beginner

spring tension curtain rod
steel tape measure
chalk marking pencil
scissors
lightweight sheer fabric
pins
iron
matching thread
 sewing machine
four narrow rods or dowels, painted
    white and cut to window width

1. Place curtain rod in window
frame at desired height.
2. Measure desired length of
curtain (from rod to sill); add 10
inches. Measure window width;
add 3 inches. Cut two fabric panels
to these measurements for each
window.
3. Turn under ½ inch, then 1 inch,
on each long edge of each panel; pin
and press. Stitch close to folds to
hem side edges.
4. Turn under ½ inch, then 3
inches, on upper and lower edge
of each panel; pin and press. Stitch
close to folds to hem upper and
lower edges.
5. Measure and mark 3 lines across
center of panel, placing first line
about 14 inches below upper edge
and remaining lines each 14 inches
below first.
6. Fold panel along each line; stitch
¾ inches from line to form pockets.
7. Insert rods or dowels through
pockets. Insert rod into top pocket
of shade and mount.

⤐ folded shade

Craft a colorful folded shade with a large sheet of heavy pastel paper. Measure and cut the paper to fit within the window frame, then fold it accordion-style. Add eyelets to each pleat and thread both sides with tasseled adjustable strings.

SKILL LEVEL: beginner

steel tape measure

large sheet of pastel paper (must be large enough to fit or be cut to fit your window width and length)

long metal ruler

pencil

craft knife or saw

cutting mat

2-inch-wide mounting board or wood slat (we used a ³/₃₂-inch-thick piece of balsa wood)

glue or glue stick

small hole punch

eyelets

eyelet tool

hammer

string

screw eyes

staple gun or wood screws and drill and driver with ¹/₈-inch bit and screwdriver bit

cord pull

shade cleat and mounting hardware

1. Measure width and length of inside window frame. Measure, mark and cut paper to dimensions ¼ inch shorter than width and 3 inches longer than length of inside window frame, using craft knife and straightedge. Cut two 1-inch-wide strips of paper equal to length of cut paper shade. Measure, mark and cut wood slat or mounting board to length ¼ inch shorter than inside frame width.

2. Spread a thin layer of glue to backs of 1-inch-wide paper strips and apply to side edges of back side of shade. On back side of shade, measure and mark lines across width of shade 1 inch apart from top to bottom. Using straightedge and back of craft knife, lightly score along each line, making sure not to cut through paper. Fold shade along scored lines in accordion pleats, sharply pressing creases.

3. Except in top pleat, punch small holes through center of 1 inch square of each pleat along both side edges. Insert eyelet through hole, place on cutting mat, and secure in place using eyelet tool and hammer—or follow manufacturer's instructions. Repeat until each hole contains a finished eyelet.

4. Making sure your string fits easily through the eyelets, cut one piece of string three times longer than and another two times longer than window frame length. Thread one piece of string through the eyelets along one side of shade, and the other piece through eyelets on other side. Knot the string at the bottom of each side, leaving a 4-inch-long tail.

5. Glue back side of top pleat to wood slat. Insert screw eyes through center of slat, ½ inch in from either end, drilling starter holes if necessary. Drill starter holes in top of window frame to accommodate screw eyes, if necessary. Install shade in window, stapling or screwing mounting slat or board to frame.

challenge: Treating a wall of stacked windows in a traditional bedroom.

solution: Painted wood shutters hung inside the frame unify large banks of windows, allowing controllable privacy in a personal space. Contemporary shutters harmonize with modern windows, turning a bedroom into a serene and cozy retreat.

6. Thread long piece of string through screw eye above, then across shade through opposite screw eye. Thread shorter string through screw eye above and let hang next to long piece. Adjust shade so it hangs evenly. Thread ends of string through a cord pull, knotting ends, and cut off excess. Install shade cleat on side of frame where desired.

7. Make tassel by wrapping string several times around three fingers to form loop. Tie loop together with string; cut loop at bottom to form tassel ends. Wrap string around tassel top a few times and knot to secure. Then tie tassel onto tails at bottoms sides of shade.

challenge: Earth-toned bathroom needs privacy and light.

solution: Natural-fiber shades add a relaxed feel to a laid-back space. They adjust easily to regulate both light and privacy, and their neutral tone and texture are organic to an indoor-outdoor aesthetic.

challenge: With the couch in front of the window, curtains are awkward, but using no treatment will fade the couch's fabric.

solution: A practical shade topped with a fashionable valance gives you the best of both worlds. The fabric's soft color plays off the bamboo's hard texture in a multilayer contrast that enlivens an informal or traditional decor.

challenge: Unfussy country kitchen needs some privacy.

solution: Rather than a traditional country look, try picking up the warm wood tones of the kitchen's pine table, chairs and accessories. For instance, these simple bamboo shades lend warmth, a bit of sophistication and a measure of privacy to the room's country style. In addition, their horizontal lines are a nice juxtaposition to the vertical lines of the bead board walls.

3

CURTAINS AND DRAPERIES

trend watch

From laid-back to luxurious, draperies are key in setting the tone of any room.

no pleats Create a clean, transitional look with rings sewn directly to the top of unpleated panels. Line the fabric panels to ensure soft, graceful folds.

borders Contrasting fabric borders add an extra level of polish to draperies made of a solid fabric without overwhelming the room with pattern. Pinch pleats, a classic heading choice, give fullness to panels.

grommets Rather than traditional rods, rings and finials, a sleek rod running through large grommets gives streamlined curtain panels a sleek, modern look.

❦ fixed-top curtains

SKILL LEVEL: intermediate to challenging

two ¾ x 4-inch boards, cut to
  desired width of each curtain
  (see Note)
hammer and long nails
cup hooks
screw eyes
steel tape measure
chalk marking pencil
decorative curtain fabric
cotton interlining fabric
cotton lining fabric
scissors
pins
iron
sewing machine
hand-sewing needle
small plastic shade rings
4-inch-wide pinch-pleat header tape
1-inch metal sew-on curtain rings
curtain or blind cord
screwdriver
cleats and screws
two shade pulls

Note: These curtains have a fixed top, and do not cover the entire window. To cover more of the window, use longer ¾ x 4s, or use a single ¾ x 4-inch board and let curtains meet in center. The curtains are finished with an Italian stringing technique, which allows the curtains to be pulled back in the center without disturbing the fixed upper edge, much like theater curtains.

1. Mount the ¾ x 4-inch board above the window at desired curtain starting point (ideally just below the molding) using hammer and nails.
2. Attach cup hooks every 2 inches along front edge of board, starting and ending near ends. Attach screw eyes to lower edge of board about two-thirds of the way from the point where the leading edge of curtain will be mounted and near the outer ends of the board (to hold guide cords for the Italian stringing).
3. Measure desired width of each panel; triple this measurement for a very full effect. Measure the desired length of each panel and add 30 inches (to allow the panels to puddle on the floor and to have a full header). Cut two pieces of decorative fabric to these measurements. Cut two pieces each of interlining and lining, each 3 inches shorter than face fabric.
4. Turn lower edges of interlining and lining panels up ½ inch, then 6 inches; pin, press; topstitch hems.
5. Place face fabric right side up; top with lining, right side down, then interlining, right side down, with upper and side edges even (lining and interlining will fall short of lower edge of face fabric). Pin and stitch upper and side edges with ½-inch seams. Trim corners and turn right side out. Press lightly on lining side.
6. On lining side, mark horizontal lines across panels 8 inches and 12 inches from upper edge. Hand-baste through all layers along both lines.
7. Mark desired starting point for Italian stringing; the one pictured started 2 feet below top of curtain. Enlarge Italian stringing pattern (see pattern and *How to Enlarge Patterns*, page 127). Place pattern on wrong side of panel, starting at marked position on front edge, and transfer marks for ring positions, adding more rings if needed for very heavy panels.
8. Hand sew a plastic ring at each position, sewing through all layers and lightly catching the face fabric in each stitch.
9. To gather the upper edges of the panels, pin pleater tape along lining side between basted lines. Turn short edge of tape under ½ inch at the leading edge of curtain, placing it slightly inside leading edge. Sew along front upper and lower edges of tape, leaving other short edge free. Pull tape cords to achieve desired panel width; secure cords and sew remaining short edge of tape down. Panels will be permanently gathered to this width.
10. Sew metal curtain rings near upper edge of tape, spacing rings 2 inches apart and placing rings near both ends of tape.
11. Mount curtains on boards. The extra 8 inches at upper edge form the softly gathered header that covers the sewing lines of gathered pleater tape. Mark desired curtain length on face fabric. Remove curtains from hooks.
12. Turn under raw lower edges of face fabric ½ inch, then turn up hem at marked points; press and blind-stitch hem in place.
13. Cut two 8-foot lengths of curtain cord. Tie cord to rings closest to leading edge on each panel and string up through remaining rings, as shown in illustration.
14. Mount curtains. String cord through screw eyes on mounting board so string hangs on outer edge.
15. Mount cleat on wall at desired height. Pull cords to open curtains, then wrap cord around cleats. Slip a shade pull onto each cord; knot ends and trim excess.

challenge: What's the best window treatment for a wall of Palladian windows?

solution: Simple side panels treat Palladian windows as architectural elements to be accented, not covered. Vertical pleats and traditional checks complement the window's classic design, drawing the eye upward to the strong arch.

challenge: A window with an arched top presented a decorating dilemma. Window treatments were needed to provide necessary privacy and light control, but their design had to be simple so that they would neither cover up this interesting architectural detail nor overwhelm the small space.

solution: Café-style curtains reach partially up the window, providing privacy without hiding the pretty window—or completely blocking out sunshine. By placing the curtains on rods that swing out, they can also be pulled out of the way entirely when so desired. Because the curtains are simply clipped to rings, they also can be switched out with the seasons with little fuss.

challenge: Treating an arch. A graceful arch window centered squarely on a wall is the architectural focal point of this formal dining room. The choice of treatment had to complement the feature, not obscure it.

solution: Elegant draperies hung with a trio of rosettes offer an uninterrupted view of the window and the vista outside. Choosing drapery fabric in a soft gold harmonizes with the pale yellow hue of the walls and keeps the focus on the window's graceful shape.

challenge: Accenting a focal point. A pretty Palladian window is the center of attention in this second-floor bedroom with breathtaking garden views. The homeowners were tempted to leave it bare, but the effect was too stark.

solution: Two sweeping drapes that pull up at the sides with decorative tassels rest at the sill and frame the window and the verdant view perfectly. The rods are concealed by deep, curvy molding that just allows the softening folds of the curtains to peep through.

challenge: What curtains would look best in a bedroom with a cathedral ceiling and a picture window?

solution: Floor-length panels hung from the ceiling make the window proportional to the room. To make a dramatic space feel intimate, use a ruffled header and warm, sunny colors. A large-print fabric keeps the elements in proportion.

challenge: Making the most of a plain window.

solution: Turn a modest window into a floor-to-ceiling focal point by placing a table and chairs or a petite desk in front of it. Frame your window vignette with swept-back floor-length draperies hung just below the ceiling.

one style, four looks

WINDOWS: A straightforward window treatment—simple pinch pleats, no trims—allows a contemporary natural fabric to fit in a traditional setting.
• The full-length panels, which break about an inch and a half on the floor, hang from a brushed and polished nickel rod.

WALLS: Contrasts—soft and hard, dark and light—add interest and elegance.
• Antiqued brown velvet above applied white-painted panels frame the room with cozy warmth and architectural interest.
• Crown molding adds a finishing touch.
• A contemporary mirror marries old and new design elements.

FLOORS: An inlaid stripe border adds a fresh note to the oak flooring.
• An air vent, covered with a decorative grille, becomes part of the decor.

WINDOWS: Crisp fabric panels give contemporary polish to the window.
• Pinch-pleated panels edged with felt hang from a dark-stained wooden rod.
• Pencil-style holdback posts gracefully gather the drapery to each side.

WALLS: A grid-like wall treatment echoes the window's divided panes.
• Reminiscent of grasscloth, the silk wallcovering offers modern flavor to a traditional setting.
• Decorative welting separates the squares; nail heads accent corners.
• The modern treatment, set off by a deeper-shaded crown molding and baseboard, is right at home with framed etchings, circa 1940.

FLOORS: Adding to the ambience, wall-to-wall carpeting in a small-scale pattern picks up on the color scheme.

WINDOWS: A wide window gets a treatment that stands up to its size.

- A voluminous taffeta window treatment covers the 6-foot expanse of windows in the dining room.
- A 6- to 7-inch puddle on the floor emphasizes the shimmery quality of the fabric.
- Wrought-iron rod and rings and birdcage finials counterpoint gilded French antique holdbacks.

WALLS: Texture plays off the other elements in the room.

- A natural woven wallcovering contrasts with silk-taffeta draperies, yet complements their iridescent color.

FLOORS: A rug introduces pattern.

- A custom square rug, featuring vines and flowers, adds formal country flavor well suited to the wooded scenery outside the window.

WINDOWS: A horizontal stripe pattern gives contemporary flavor to silk-taffeta draperies.

- Brass holdbacks let the panels drape ever so softly, goblet pleats lend polish.
- Hung high, the draperies add height.

WALLS: Money-saving paint techniques lend affordable character and texture.

- Applied baseboard, crown molding and a chair rail introduce architectural accents.
- A square of paneling beneath the window makes the window look as if it goes all the way to the floor like a French door.
- A faux paint-and-glaze treatment—with very fine ragging— gives the walls a paneled look.

FLOORS: Oak flooring forms a beautiful backdrop for a flat-weave carpet.

- The reproduction art deco Aubusson rug contrasts softly with the crisp draperies.

SHEERS

❧ flower curtains

These easy, breezy curtains give any room petal power.
Hang them in a bathroom or bedroom to provide filtered privacy
or anywhere you want to add a lighthearted lift.

NO SEW
SKILL LEVEL: beginner

clean sheets of paper
two sheer window panels
fabric flowers
fabric glue

1. Cover floor with paper and lay one sheer panel on top. Smooth out wrinkles.
2. Remove stems and leaves from flowers. Arrange flowers as desired on panel and glue in place. Let dry one hour.
3. If any flowers stick to paper, gently loosen before hanging. Repeat with second panel.

❦ tailored sheer panels

Filter light while adding beauty to your windows with these tailored sheer panels. To let in light without traditional tiebacks, simply gather the material up into a loose knot. Or you can tie on a raffia bow and insert some fresh flowers for an inspired summer display.

SKILL LEVEL: beginner

steel tape measure
metal ruler
chalk marking pencil
sheer fabric
scissors
lining fabric
matching thread
sewing machine
pins
hand-sewing needle
sticky-back hook and loop tape
iron

1. Measure width of outside window frame, add 4 inches and divide by 2. Measure from top of window frame to floor and add 3 inches. Measure, mark and cut two sheer-fabric panels to these dimensions.

2. For top band, measure, mark and cut two strips from sheer fabric and one strip from lining fabric, measuring 4½-inch-wide times the width of window frame plus 1 inch.

3. Turn under and press a ½-inch double-fold hem along both side edges of both panels. Stitch in place with blind hemstitch. Turn under and press a 2-inch double fold hem along bottom. Stitch in place with blind hemstitch.

4. Place lining on back side of one sheer top band, pin and baste. Place panels side by side, right sides up, on work surface. Center long edge of basted top band, face down, over top edges of panels, matching raw edges. Pin in place; stitch top band to panels.

5. Cut a strip of hook-and-loop tape equal in length to window frame width. Peel off backing and attach loop portion of strip along center of right side of remaining top piece. Attach hook portion of tape along center of window frame top.

6. Position remaining top piece over basted top piece, right sides facing, raw edges matching; pin in place. Sew around both short edges, and long edge that's not attached to panels with a ½-inch seam allowance. Clip corners. Turn top piece right side out and press, fold under and press raw edge; hand stitch opening closed. Connect hook and loop strips to attach to window.

challenge: The bed positioning. It can only be beneath two high windows. How can the bed and the windows work together?

solution: Consider the windows an extension of the headboard, both in design and in color, giving them a simple style that complements the feminine bed frame and linens. Here, stationary white sheers, topped with a delicate swag that repeats the linens' primary color, create the sense of a canopy. For design continuity, the sheers are subtly adorned with a fern pattern, as are the linens. The swag also serves to hide rolled-up window shades necessary for privacy and light control.

gathered sheers

SKILL LEVEL: beginner

spring tension curtain rod
steel tape measure
chalk marking pencil
scissors
lightweight sheer fabric
pins
iron
matching thread
sewing machine

1. Place curtain rod in window frame at desired height.

2. Measure desired length of curtain (from rod to sill); add 9 inches. Measure window width; add 4 inches. Cut two fabric panels to these measurements for each window.

3. Turn under ½ inch, then 1 inch, on each long edge of each panel; pin and press. Stitch close to folds to hem side edges.

4. Turn under ½ inch, then 4 inches, on upper and lower edge of each panel; pin and press. Stitch close to folds to hem upper and lower edges.

5. Mark a line across upper edge of each panel, about 2 inches below fold, depending upon desired ruffle width. Stitch along marked line.

6. Insert rod through pocket formed below ruffle.

flower-cascade curtain

NO SEW

SKILL LEVEL: beginner

curtain rod: standard; 2½-inch wide, flat; 2½-inch wide, flat tension

fabric in desired amount

steel tape measure

scissors

iron

Velcro brand Fabric Fusion tape (no-sew)

fabric flowers

Velcro brand Sticky Back tape

grosgrain ribbon

Note: If covering an oversize window, fuse two or more fabric panels together.

1. Install rod. Turn top edge of fabric down 1 inch; iron on loop section of Fabric Fusion tape.

2. Fuse a 4-inch double hem on bottom edge.

3. Apply flowers to fabric by ironing on small loop pieces of Fabric Fusion tape randomly across the fabric and hook pieces to back of a flower petals.

4. Apply hook section of Sticky Back tape to rod. Attach curtain to rod, rippling top to fit. Tie back with ribbon.

shimmering sheers

To create these delicate panels, buy a few sheer place mats, overlap their edges, stitch them together, add clips and mount them on a rod.

SKILL LEVEL: beginner

steel tape measure

four or more sheer decorative placemats

pins

matching thread

sewing machine

hand-sewing needle (optional)

curtain clips

tension rod

1. Measure the width and height of your window to determine the number of place mats you'll need to join to cover one-half to two-thirds of your window with a flat panel. When making your calculation, remember that the place mat borders will overlap in the center.

2. Pin two place mats together, overlapping two short edges, right sides facing up. Topstitch along both edges of the overlapping borders to join the panels. Repeat with two more panels, and two more, if necessary. If you want to stack two pairs of three place mats with the long edges running vertically, topstitch another place mat along the other short edge of one pair of joined panels, then repeat for the other pair. Remove pins.

3. Overlap the long edges of the joined panels, pinning in place. Topstitch along one edge of the overlapped borders, rolling over excess fabric to flow smoothly through the machine as you sew. If the layers are too thick for your sewing machine needle to pass through where all four borders overlap, lift the sewing machine foot, slide this section forward and start sewing again where only two sections overlap. Remove pins. Hand sew the central section closed with a slip-stitch, if necessary.

4. Apply curtain clips, evenly spaced, along either the long or short edge of panel as desired, then slide rings over rod. Install rod into place in window frame.

THE HERMITAGE, LENINGRAD:
FRENCH 19th CENTURY MASTERS

A HISTORY OF ART

ARCH

Art through the Ages

DICTIONARY OF

IMPRESSIONISTS   SCOTT REYBURN

Crown

challenge: This dining room is decorated in a formal, traditional style. How do you use simple sheer panels, yet give them some zing at the same time?

solution: Tied tab tops give these unstuffy sheers a subtle contemporary touch, as does hanging them from a black wrought-iron rod, installed about 12 inches above the top of the window. Tabs also let you pull them back easily to reveal the view. But what really gives these panels some flair is the fabric's subtle gold sunburst pattern, which picks up the tones of the brass chandelier and the mirror frames.

challenge: Airy sheers can make a plain window seem even plainer. How can they be dressed up?

solution: A lightweight cornice adds a dressy detail, while retaining the airy feel. Embellishing the cornice with an elegant scalloped hem and a drawn-on design preserves the classic color scheme. Carrying the motif to the room's other furnishings ties the space together.

challenge: Large French doors and small windows. How can they appear more in proportion in this bathroom?

solution: Dress the bathtub surround facing the windows with a sheer light-filtering swag and sunny curtains hung at ceiling height. Mirror the treatment on the French doors to give the elements the same visual weight.

tab-topped panels

It's easy to craft a pair of tab-topped panels. The graceful solid border contains a meandering floral pattern, and simple tie-top closures allow you to remove the panels for cleaning without taking down the rod.

SKILL LEVEL: beginner

steel tape measure

metal ruler

chalk marking pencil

decorator fabrics—one print, one solid

scissors

iron

pins

matching thread

sewing machine

needle

1. Measure length from 1 inch below rod to sill and width of outside window frame. Measure, mark and cut two panels of decorator fabric to these measurements plus 1 inch.

2. Add 7 inches to the length measurement and 13 inches to the width measurement and cut two panels from contrasting fabric to these dimensions.

3. Turn under and press 3½ inches along all sides of each of the larger panels toward wrong side of fabric. Turn and press ½ inch along long edges of smaller panels toward wrong side. Center smaller panel over larger, right sides facing. Pin long raw edges together and stitch in place. Repeat for other panel. Turn both panels right side out. Fold under and press ½ inch along raw edges of top and bottom of larger panels; then fold edges over 3 inches to form borders. Fold in corners to miter; pin. Topstitch inner folded edges and mitered corners.

4. To make tie, cut a strip of fabric 1 x 12 inches. Fold tie in half lengthwise and press. Open tie, and fold in raw edges ¼ inch and press. Refold along first crease. Topstitch all around. Repeat for all ties—you should make enough ties for each panel to be spaced 6 to 8 inches apart, beginning and ending at side edges.

5. Press each tie in half crosswise, then open tie and pin folded edge in place at one side of panel ¼ inch below top. Repeat on other side. Continue pinning ties along top edge, evenly spacing them 6 to 8 inches apart. Repeat for other panel. Topstitch along top edge of both panels to secure ties in place.

❧ reversible curtains

Use iron-on fusible web to create these charming reversible curtains. Grosgrain ribbon loops add whimsy and let you pull back the corners to reveal both fabrics.

NO SEW

SKILL LEVEL: beginner

curtain rod and mounting hardware

screw driver or drill driver

steel measuring tape

two kinds of complementary decorator fabric

long metal ruler

chalk marking pencil

scissors

iron

½-inch-wide grosgrain or other cloth ribbon

⅝-inch-wide fusible iron-on web (we used Therm O Web's Heat N Bond)

drawer pulls

1. Mount curtain rod where desired above window frame.

2. Measure width outside window frame and length from just below curtain rod to window sill. Divide width by 2 and add 1¼ inches to length measurement. Measure, mark and cut two panels from each fabric to these dimensions.

3. Turn in and press side, bottom and top edges of all panels ⅝ inch. Trim all corners on diagonal ¼ inch from folds. Turn in and press cut corners ¼ inch.

4. Measure the diameter of your curtain rod and multiply by 3½, add 1½ inches. Cut strips of grosgrain or other ribbon to this length for curtain loops. You should cut enough strips for each finished panel to be spaced about 6 to 8 inches apart, beginning and ending at side edges, plus two more for corner pull-backs.

5. Fold loops in half. Cut twice as many ½-inch-wide pieces of fusible web as you have pieces of ribbon. Following manufacturer's instructions, iron on web to inside of free end of each loop. Press inside of remaining free end to the web to close each loop, then iron a piece of web on outside of each closed loop near cut ends.

6. Cut two strips of web equal to width and length of finished panel for each panel. Following manufacturer's instructions, iron on strips of web to folded edges of front piece of each panel. Peel paper backing off web strips on each panel and off loops. Starting at side edges, evenly space loops along top edge with web side of loop facing up and raw edges aligned. Position reverse side of panel on top, aligning folded edges, and press top edge until all pieces are secured in place. (You may have to press longer if your fabric is fairly heavy.) Position a loop at the outer lower corner of your panel, web side up, and continue pressing all around until your panel is completely secured. Repeat for other panel.

7. Thread your panels onto rod and mount. Draw back inner corners toward wall to determine placement of drawer pulls on your wall. Mark the point with a pencil and screw in pulls. Loop pull backs over drawer pulls.

challenge: What's a good way to dress a window in an attic bedroom? There is a shade for privacy, but how can it be softened and the window tied in with the room's decor. Sloping windows can be tricky, since window treatments will naturally fall away from the wall at an obvious angle.

solution: Try holding draperies in place with a full-width rod attached at the bottom of the window at both sides. The drapery shown here is attached at top by simple tabs, and can be pulled closed to block light. Stationary panels can also be installed along the sides and held in place with decorative holdbacks. Just be sure the holdback is sturdy and installed securely to bear the weight of the fabric without pulling away from the wall. For a romantic look, use lacy or sheer panels installed across the window; vary the rod to complement the look.

challenge: Blinds are great for their simplicity, how do you get something softer in a bathroom?

solution: Sheer café curtains give you privacy and let in light without overdressing the windows. Hang them full—twice the width of the window—to add a billowy softness.

❧ sunny café curtains

Craft some cheerful café curtains by stitching ribbon onto the raw edges of three napkins or start from scratch with a couple yards of fabric.

NO SEW
SKILL LEVEL: beginner

curtain rod and mounting hardware

three 20-inch square napkins or cotton fabric

yardstick

scissors

matching thread

sewing machine

seam sealant (we used Fray Check)

ribbon in two colors as desired, ½ inch wide and 2 inches wide

fusible hem tape: ½ inch wide, 2 inches wide

iron

curtain clips

1. Mount curtain rod in window at desired height.

2. Measure desired length of curtain (starting about 1½ inches below rod to allow for ring length); if you're working with fabric add 2 inches to this measurement. Measure width of window; if you're working with fabric divide this measurement in half and add 4 inches.

3. Open the hem on one side of two of the napkins. To make your panels the correct length, subtract the length of the opened napkin from the desired length of the curtain and cut two borders from the third napkin to this dimension, making sure three sides of the border have hemmed edges. Clean finish the unhemmed edges with a wide zigzag stitch or apply Fray Check or another seam sealant along unhemmed edges.

If using fabric, cut two curtain panels to the Step 2 measurements.

4. Cut two pieces of each ribbon to width of each curtain plus one inch. Stitch the wide ribbon along one unhemmed edge of each napkin, folding ends over to back at edges. Stitch other side of ribbon to borders to complete the panels. Sew other ribbon to border about ½ inch from first ribbon. If using fabric, sew ribbon borders on first, turn sides under ½ inch, then ½ inch again; press. Sew side hems in place. Turn under and press upper and lower edges and sew in place in same manner to finish hemming curtains.

5. Attach clips to upper edges of curtains, placing one at each upper corner and spacing remaining clips evenly about 6 inches apart. Hang curtains on rod.

❧ kitchen café curtains

The decorative tabs on these colorful café curtains are actually two layers of ribbon looped large enough to slide easily along the rod.

NO SEW

SKILL LEVEL: beginner

---

steel tape measure

chalk marking pencil

Kirsch Antique Pewter Faucet finials, curtain rod and brackets to fit window width

drill

fabric

air-soluble fabric marker

scissors

iron

HeatnBond ⅝-inch-wide Ultrahold fusible tape

2-inch and ⅝-inch ribbon in coordinating colors

pins

Velcro brand Fabric Fusion tape

wooden dragonfly cutouts

paintbrushes

acrylic paints and permanent markers in assorted colors

Velcro brand Sticky-Back Coins

Note: We railroaded fabric, with selvage parallel to windowsill.

A vibrant print and playful ribbon loops make a cute combo in these kitchen café curtains. Colorful dragonfly cutouts bring a touch of whimsy (like the ribbons, they're removable for washing), and wooden blinds add a textural design note and needed privacy.

1. Measure and mark desired position of rod, center and install.

2. Measure length of rod; multiply by 2½, then divide in half to obtain width of each fabric panel. Measure distance from rod to sill and subtract 1½ inches for finished length of curtain. Add 12 inches to this measurement (for a 4-inch double bottom hem and 1½-inch double top hem). Mark and cut fabric to desired length. If panels need to be joined to achieve desired width, fuse together, right sides facing, with HeatnBond, following manufacturer's instructions.

3. Turn in 1½-inch double hem on each short edge of each panel; press. Fuse HeatnBond tape between layers, close to edge of hem.

4. Turn up 4-inch double hem on lower edge of each panel toward wrong side; press. Fuse HeatnBond tape between layers, close to edge of hem.

5. Turn under 1½-inch double hem on upper edge of each panel; press.

6. Apply HeatnBond tape to inner edge of upper hem, but do not remove release paper.

7. Pin or mark placement of ribbon ties, evenly spaced about 8 inches apart, on wrong side of upper edge of panels between the two ribbons that will be placed at ends.

8. Fuse HeatnBond to wrong side of narrow ribbon; remove paper to fuse narrow ribbon to center of wide ribbon. Cut 18-inch lengths of layered ribbon for each mark. Trim ribbon ends into points.

9. Cut 3 inches of Velcro brand Fabric Fusion tape for each mark. Pin hook side of 3-inch sections perpendicular to upper edge on right side of panel at each mark. Fuse tape in place from wrong side of fabric. Remove pins.

10. Place panels right side up; open up top hem; remove release paper from HeatnBond along upper edge. Place ribbons right side up on panel front at each mark, raw edges even with top raw edge. Fold back hems and ribbons; fuse in place.

11. Insert short pieces of HeatnBond between ribbon and hem as needed; fuse to secure hem.

12. Fold ribbons toward front of panel into loops large enough to slide along rod. (Place curtain on rod, and adjust loops as needed, before pinning.) Pin 3-inch loop section of Velcro brand Fabric Fusion tape to wrong side of loose end of each ribbon. Fuse strips to ribbons, starting at pins and working toward ribbon points. Remove pins.

13. Paint wooden dragonflies; let dry. Add details with markers.

14. Apply hook sections of Velcro brand Sticky-Back Coins to backs of dragonflies. Cut matching circles of loop section of Velcro brand Fabric Fusion tape and fuse to ribbons where desired. Press dragonflies onto ribbons.

❦ café curtain

SKILL LEVEL: beginner

café curtain tension rod or
    decorative drawer pulls

steel tape measure

pencil

drill and slim drill bit (optional)

gingham fabric

chalk marking pencil

scissors

iron

matching thread

sewing machine

pins

³/₄-inch-wide flat braid trim

¹/₂-inch-wide ribbon

Fray-Check liquid or other seam
    sealant

1. Mount rod in window at desired height. Or mark positions of drawer pulls, evenly spaced, on window frame and drill starter holes and screw in pulls.

2. Determine window width; multiply this measurement by 1½ for curtain width. Measure desired length of curtain from rod or knobs to windowsill. Measure, mark and cut fabric to these measurements.

3. Turn under ½-inch double fold on upper edge of curtain; press. Stitch close to pressed edge to make upper hem.

4. With curtain right side up, fold up ½ inch on lower and side edges, so raw edges are facing up; press, folding in fullness at corners.

5. Pin braid trim along lower and side edges, covering raw edges of gingham and folding mitered angles at corners. Let braid extend ½ inch above upper hem on both side edges. Stitch close to both edges of trim, turning under ½ inch at upper hem.

6. Mark placement of ribbon ties along upper hem, placing one tie at each end and spacing remaining ties evenly about 6 inches apart along hem. Cut a 12-inch piece of ribbon for each tie. Apply Fray-Check liquid or other seam sealant to cut edges of ties; let dry.

7. Place curtain wrong side up. Pin center of tie at each mark; stitch through centers along upper edge of curtain.

8. To mount curtain, tie bows about 2 inches above upper edge of curtain and slip along rod or knobs.

❧ graceful draped curtains

Add an elegant touch with a row of beaded trim.

NO SEW

SKILL LEVEL: beginner

curtain rod: standard; 2½-inch wide, flat; 2½-inch wide, flat tension

steel tape measure

fabric in desired amount

scissors

Velcro brand Fabric Fusion tape (no-sew)

iron

Velcro brand Sticky Back tape

rust-proof straight pins

sewing machine

hand-sewing needle

beaded trim

1. Install rod. Measure from floor to top edge of rod, across rod and down to floor. Add 2 feet to measurement for hems and puddling. Measure, mark and cut fabric to these measurements.

2. Fuse 4-inch double bottom hems and 1½-inch double side hems.

3. Find center top of window treatment; iron on a strip of the loop section of Fabric Fusion tape along edge to equal width of rod.

4. Apply hook section of Sticky Back tape to the upper edge of wrong side of rod.

5. Fan-fold fabric; tie in place at corners with string.

6. Join hook and loop tapes. Adjust swag and hand sew beaded trim in place.

❧ tall pleated draperies

Floor-to-ceiling pleated draperies add understated softness to a petite living room window.
Pleated linen panels were paired with a textured shade—both in the same creamy hue as
the walls—letting subtle differences in weave and sheen provide quiet contrast. Thin rings
and a refined iron rod hung at molding-height let the fine fabrics and woodwork shine.

SKILL LEVEL: beginner

---

curtain rod and mounting hardware
steel tape measure
chalk marking pencil
curtain fabric
scissors
pins
iron
matching thread
sewing machine
4-inch-wide pinch-pleat header tape
sew-on curtain rings (to match rod)
hand-sewing needle

---

1. Mount rod above window.

2. Measure the width of each window and multiply by 1½. Measure the desired length of fabric panel and add 11 inches. Cut each of the two fabric panels to these measurements.

3. Turn side edges of each panel under ½ inch, then 3 inches; pin and press, then topstitch side hems in place. Turn lower edge of each panel under ½ inch, then 6 inches; pin and press, then topstitch hems in place. Turn upper edge of each panel under ½ inch, then 4 inches; pin and press, then topstitch hems in place.

4. To create pleats along the upper edges of the panels, pin pleater tape along upper hem on wrong side. Turn short edge of tape under ½ inch at leading edge of curtain so it's positioned slightly away from curtain edge. Sew along leading short edge and upper and lower edges of tape, leaving back edge free. Pull tape cords to achieve desired pleating; secure cords and sew remaining edge of tape down.

5. Hand sew curtain rings near upper edge of each panel, placing a ring near each end and behind each pleat.

6. Mount curtain panels on rod.

These linen draperies almost blend in to the wall, while still being functional. They are mounted on sleek metal curtain rods finished in antique silver and custom-made so their ends turn to merge with the wall.

76 ❧ CURTAINS AND DRAPERIES

challenge: French doors need covering at night. What kind of window treatment would look formal but not terribly fussy?

solution: Floor-length panels hung above the frame provide easy access. A subtle floral pattern visually links the garden beyond, creating a transition from indoors to out. Adjoining windows can be drawn into the treatment for a cohesive look.

For this bedroom, a shade of fawn was chosen for the walls, a light accent color for the ceiling and a mid-tone color for the trim. The fabric of the draperies complements this palette.

❧ wide-stripe curtains

Handsome wide stripes accentuate tall ceilings and offer a modern touch to a traditional yet contemporary room.

SKILL LEVEL: beginner

curtain rod and mounting hardware
drill with drill and screwdriver bits
steel tape measure
chalk marking pencil
lining fabric
curtain fabric
scissors
iron
pins
matching thread
sewing machine
1-inch metal sew-on curtain rings
hand-sewing needle

1. Mount rod above window.

2. Measure the width of the window and multiply by 2½. Measure the desired length of fabric panels. Measure, mark and cut two pieces of lining to these dimensions. Add 7 inches to width measurement and add 13 inches to length measurement. Measure, mark and cut each fabric panel to these measurements.

3. Turn side edges of each fabric panel under ½ inch, then 3 inches; press. Unfold curtain fabric edges, center lining fabric over curtain fabric, wrong sides facing, fold back hems to conceal raw edges of lining; pin, then topstitch side hems in place. Turn upper and lower edges of each panel under ½ inch, then 6 inches; pin and press, then topstitch hems in place.

4. Hand sew metal curtain rings along upper edge of panels, evenly spacing rings about 6 inches apart and placing rings near both ends of each panel.

5. Mount curtains on rod, and attach to brackets.

challenge: Integrating a corner window. The wraparound windows in this living room overlook a neighbor's property. Plus, they're two different sizes. The owners wanted a treatment that would offer privacy and harmonize with their elegant room decor.

solution: The windows are artfully united with simple, floor-length panels. Hung about 6 inches above the frame, the cream-colored folds create the elegant illusion of architectural columns. Wrought-iron rods accent the clean angular lines of the windows. When the panels are closed, the fabric draws the eye up to the cathedral ceiling and its striking Fortuny silk lamp.

LAYERED LOOKS

❦ cotton floral drapes

Bring spring inside with these delightful floral drapes. The large graphic print, combined with a smaller print and stripes, keeps the look from becoming too sweet. Solid colors on the floor, sofa and pillows tie the room together perfectly.

SKILL LEVEL: beginner

---

curtain rod and mounting hardware

screwdriver

yardstick

chalk marking pencil

scissors

cotton fabrics in three prints: large
    floral, small floral and striped

matching thread

sewing machine

iron

1. Mount curtain rod above window as desired.

2. Measure desired length of drapes; add 8 inches. Measure width of window; add 3 inches. Mark and cut two pieces of large floral fabric, one piece of small floral fabric and one piece of striped fabric to these measurements.

3. Turn under ½ inch, then 1 inch, on each long edge of each panel; press. Stitch close to folds to hem side edges.

4. Turn under ½ inch, then 3 inches, on lower edge of each panel; press. Stitch close to folds to hem edges.

5. Turn under ½ inch, then 4 inches, on upper edge of each panel; press. Stitch close to folds to form pockets.

6. Slip panels onto rod, starting and ending with the large floral print.

Layered looks not only add polish to windows, they're multifunctional, too, providing privacy and insulation, while mixing colors and patterns to pull any room together. Enrich them further with unique details or character-filled extras—such as finials, trims, tiebacks and distinctive headers—and even the simplest treatment becomes one-of-a-kind. Pair a Roman shade with curtain panels, layer sheers under lined draperies or combine a woven shade with a fabric one and your windows will look twice—or even thrice—as nice.

challenge: In this tiny guest room, the best place to put the bed is under the dormer window. How can this arrangement look planned instead of awkward?

solution: Make the window curtains do double-duty as a canopy. Instead of hanging them at the window, hang the valance and side panels from a tension rod that's installed between the narrow walls. Pulling the rod out a foot or two from the head of the bed will create the enclosed feeling of a canopy and give that tiny bed a real sense of prominence. A matching balloon shade on the window provides privacy and, when pulled down, a coordinating backdrop. For variety, experiment with linens and curtains in contrasting colors and patterns, customizing the look to suit the room's occupants.

Spicy earth tones, hand-printed paisley hemp linen and a wide batik border come together with a woven-wood shade in an exotic blend of color and pattern. To keep it from being busy, tailored ring-top panels were designed to flow seamlessly into the matching fabric-covered wall. As a final trick, a carved console is centered between them to give a small window presence.

❧ floor-to-ceiling draperies

Rich and stately, these draperies make a sweeping statement in a living room. For dramatic contrast cornices from metal planters turned upside down and painted matte black were created. Natural bamboo shades were added for privacy and sun control.

NO SEW

SKILL LEVEL: beginner

---

pencil

two rectangular metal planters

drill

ruler

scissors

Velcro brand Sticky-Back tape

heavy-duty picture wire

4 heavy-duty picture hooks (with anchors, if needed)

steel tape measure

fabric

HeatnBond UltraHold $3/8$-inch fusible adhesive tape

iron

Velcro brand Fabric Fusion tape

---

1. Mark position of two holes along one long side of planter near bottom corners (bottom of planter will become roof of cornice). Drill holes at marks.
2. Measure circumference of planter and cut three or four strips of hook sections of Velcro brand Sticky-Back tape to this length. Placing them adjacent to each other, press around inside of planter, leaving holes open; let adhesive cure overnight.
3. To make hanger, cut 5 feet of picture wire; thread through holes several times and twist ends together.
4. Hold planter (bottom side up) against wall at desired height; mark position of holes for placement of hooks. Attach hooks at marks. Hang planter from wire on hooks.
5. Measure from inside top of planter to floor; add 12 inches to obtain panel length. Cut full width of fabric to this length for each panel.
6. Apply HeatnBond tape to side edges of panels, placing it on wrong side of selvage along inner (leading) panel edges and on right side of selvage along outer panel edges.
7. Place panel right side up. At inner panel edge, turn in $1/2$ inch, then $3\frac{1}{4}$ inches, so wrong side of fabric shows at leading edge. Fuse this edge, stopping about 9 inches from bottom edge.
8. Turn panel wrong side up. Turn outer panel edge in $1/2$ inch, then $3\frac{1}{4}$ inches, folding right side of fabric over wrong side. Fuse this edge, stopping about 9 inches from lower edge. Measure 8 inches up from bottom on outer edge of panel, and snip 4 inches into side edge.
9. Place panel right side up. At lower edge, fold up $3\frac{1}{4}$ inches, then $3\frac{1}{4}$ inches again, to form double hem. Trim away excess fabric at hem at each lower corner.
10. Fuse HeatnBond tape along upper edge of bottom hem band. Press to fuse bottom hem.
11. Turn under remaining side edge hems and fuse to complete hems.
12. With panel wrong side up, turn upper edge over 1 inch, then 3 inches; press. Open out hem.
13. Cut, apply and fuse three or four strips of loop section of Velcro brand Fabric Fusion tape to right side of drape, placing them adjacent to each other below the folded hem line and parallel to upper cut edge along the width of the drape. Cut and apply HeatnBond to right side of 1-inch allowance and fuse in place.
14. Turn hem back in, forming a 3-inch hem, and fuse to close hem.
15. Attach panels inside planters. Start near wall on outer edge of planter, then form gentle folds in panels as you work toward wall on inner edge of planter, pressing pleats into tape inside planter and making sure fabric touches on all sides.

RIGHT: Luxurious ring-top panels with soft box pleats in a gunmetal silk add a bold finish to a neutral living space. A sheer, silvery floral-patterned balloon shade echoes the curves of pottery and wood accessories, softening the room and providing semi-privacy. For extra polish, the shade was embellished with a decorative gathered header and the finialed pole was faux-painted with metallic washes.

OPPOSITE: Flat Burberry-look taffeta panels are mounted on a narrow rod in a flap-back tent style to show off the unconventional red velvet lining. Rosettes on the British tan ribbon braiding on the leading edges of both sides echo the medallion holdbacks; a bamboo undershade controls light without blocking it completely.

❧ sun-toned roman shades

*These decorative shades provide an important function: giving privacy when needed,
while offering a handsome counterpoint to flowing floral rod pocket panels.*

SKILL LEVEL: intermediate

steel tape measure

chalk marking pencil

medium-weight gold fabric

interfacing

lining fabric

scissors

pins

matching thread

sewing machine

iron

curtain ring tape

1/2-inch-wide fusible hem tape

hand-sewing needle

self-adhesive hook-and-loop tape

1 x 1-inch wood, cut 1/2 inch shorter
     than inner width of window

3 screw eyes

shade cord or thin cotton cord

drill

2-inch wood screws

1/2-inch wood dowel, cut 1 inch
     shorter than inner width of
     window

cord pull

cleat and mounting hardware

1. Measure width of window; add 1/2 inch. Measure length of window;
add 4 inches. Cut fabric, interfacing and lining to these measurements.

2. Pin fabric to lining, with right sides facing and raw edges even. Pin
interfacing over fabric. Sew sides and lower edge with 1/2-inch seams through
all three layers. Trim corners; turn right side out. Press. Turn upper raw edges
in 1/2 inch; press and topstitch closed.

3. Turn lower edge up 2 inches; press. Cut three pieces of ring tape, each as
long as finished shade, making sure 2 inches of tape extend below the first
ring on each piece. Cut three pieces of fusible hem tape to this length.

4. Measure and mark ring tape placement as follows: Mark a line along
the length of the shade about 1 inch from each long edge and down center.
Center fusible hem tape, then ring tape, over each line, positioning bottom
rings 1 inch above the top of the hemline, sandwiching tape under the
pressed hem. Rings should align on all three pieces. Fuse in place.

5. For extra strength, handstitch top of each ring through lining and face
fabric.

6. Handstitch or machine hemstitch lower hem in place.

7. Cut hook-and-loop tape to shade width. Separate sections; attach loop
section to lining side of upper edge of shade. Attach hook section to one
long edge of wood.

8. Attach screw eyes to opposite long edge of wood, spacing them in
alignment with rings on shade.

9. Cut three pieces of cord, each twice as long as window length. Tie a cord
to bottom ring in one row, then slip cord up through each ring in sequence.
(For deeper pleats when shade is raised, you may wish to slip the cord
through alternate rings only.) Tie and thread cord through each row of rings
in same manner.

10. Press hook-and-loop tape sections together to attach shade to wood with
screw eyes facing down. Slip each cord through screw eye directly above it.

11. Determine which side of window you wish cords to hang. Slip opposite
and center cord through other rings across top so all cords hang on this side.

12. Drill four holes, evenly spaced, through wood piece and top of shade
between screw eyes, and screw wood to top of window frame. Slip dowel into
lower hem of shade so it hangs evenly.

13. Slip cord ends through pull; knot about halfway down window.
Trim excess cord.

14. Screw cleat to wall about halfway down window. Pull cords to raise
shade to desired height; wrap around cleat.

Turn to page 94 for instructions on how to make the floral rod pocket panels.

❧ rod pocket panels

SKILL LEVEL: beginner

curtain rod and mounting hardware
steel tape measure
chalk marking pencil
curtain fabric
scissors
pins
iron
matching thread
sewing machine

1. Mount rod above window.

2. Measure the width of window frame and multiply by 1½. Measure the desired length of panel and add 14 inches. Cut each of the two fabric panels to these measurements.

3. Turn side edges of each panel under ½ inch, then 3 inches; pin and press, then topstitch side hems in place. Turn under ½ inch, then 6 inches, on lower edge of each panel; pin and press, then stitch hems in place. Turn under ½ inch, then 7 inches, on upper edge of each panel; pin and press, then stitch hems in place.

4. Stitch again 3 inches above upper hem to form rod pocket and ruffle top.

5. Mount curtain on rod.

Traditional silk panels with tassels are layered with casual pin-dot woven sheers and a bamboo shade. The ensemble is topped off with chunky wood rings and a faux bamboo pole. Three totally different elements and textures melded together create an eclectic look.

trend watch: window toppings

Use rings on a decorative rod to hold a panel valance in place. Add shades that lower from the top to let in light yet still retain a feeling of privacy.

Functional and attractive, this cornice creates the look of architectural molding atop windows.

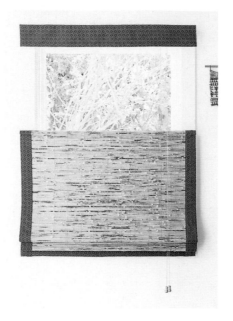

A fabric-covered pelmet adds a colorful touch to a bamboo shade edged with a border made of the same fabric.

Whether it's a draped valance, a fabric-covered cornice or a stiffened pelmet, a window topper adds a grace note to your decor. Although these terms may be used interchangeably, valances are usually thought of as elements that offer a softer, fuller effect. They might range from a swagged swath of fabric flanked with flowing cascades, to a simple cloth panel mounted with rings, to a rod across a window. Cornices and pelmets, on the other hand, are often regarded as decorative devices that provide an architectural look.

Valances, pelmets and cornices can stand alone as a crowning touch. Or they may add dimension and conceal the drapery hardware of layered window treatments that can range from Roman shades or wood blinds, to elegant floor-length drapery panels.

Window treatments are simpler and more streamlined today than they were in the 1990s, when excessive window toppings and elaborately draped valances were popular. Upholstered cornice boards—a window treatment popular in the 1950s—are making a comeback. They can have a very tailored look with contemporary furniture. A 12-inch cornice board nicely fills the space between lower and upper windows in a great room, adding a human scale without covering up the view.

TOP, RIGHT: Move away from the straight and narrow with a curved valance. Pair it with a Roman shade in a complementary fabric for a simple, summery look

RIGHT: A softly folded panel valance with café curtains makes for a classically easy window treatment.

VALANCES

❧ dotted draperies and valance

Tailored and chic, these window treatments bring living room elegance to a master bedroom. The deep-pleated valance offers a custom look, and delicate sheers (see page 100 for instructions) provide light-filtering privacy and a hint of flirty romance.

NO SEW

SKILL LEVEL: advanced

$4\frac{1}{2}$-inch-wide curtain rods (Note: We used three rods, the long rod is equal to length of finished valance, the short ones equal to finished width of panels)

drill

Velcro brand Sticky-Back tape

scissors

steel tape measure

air-soluble fabric marker

fabric

HeatnBond $\frac{3}{8}$-inch UltraHold fusible tape

iron

pins

masking tape

Velcro brand Fabric Fusion tape

seam sealant

Velcro brand Sticky-Back coins

---

1. Install rod(s) below ceiling at desired positions beyond window frame. (Note: Our short rods are mounted at angles along sloped edges framing window. If you don't have angled walls, mount short rods an inch below long rod flush with ends.)
2. Remove rods from brackets. Apply three rows of hook sections of Velcro brand Sticky-Back tape along back of each short rod, 1 inch apart. Apply two rows of hook sections of Velcro brand Sticky-Back tape along back of long rod, 1 inch apart.
3. Measure distance from top of short rods to floor at each end of each rod. For draperies, add $11\frac{1}{2}$ inches to longest measurement (if your panels will be mounted at angles) and cut panels to this length. If several widths of fabric need to be joined to achieve desired width, place right sides of panels facing, then fuse edges with HeatnBond (follow manufacturer's instructions), starting tape at top and stopping $6\frac{1}{2}$ inches from bottom.
4. Clip seam allowance, then join remaining $6\frac{1}{2}$ inches with wrong sides facing.
(Note: The bottom edge of our drapery has a $3\frac{1}{4}$-inch-wide contrasting band formed by folding the fabric to the right side to make a double hem equal to the size of our pattern repeat. If you have a patterned fabric, and the flip side is not attractive, fold your hems to the wrong side of the fabric and forego contrasting borders. If you do this, in Step 3, fuse adjoining widths along entire length of panels, and in the following steps, place fusible tape on the side of the fabric that will allow you to fold the hems to the backs of the panels.)
5. Apply HeatnBond tape to side edges of panels, placing tape on wrong side of fabric at inner (leading) edge and on right side of fabric at outer edge.
6. Place panel right side up. Turn inner panel edge in $\frac{1}{2}$ inch, then $3\frac{1}{4}$ inches, so wrong side of fabric folds over right side. Fuse this edge, stopping about 9 inches from lower edge.
7. Turn panel wrong side up. Turn outer panel edge in $\frac{1}{2}$ inch, then $3\frac{1}{4}$ inches, so right side of fabric folds over wrong side. Fuse this edge, stopping about 9 inches from lower edge. On outer side edge of panel, measure up 8 inches from the bottom cut edge and snip 4 inches into side edge.
8. Turn panel right side up. At lower edge, fold up $3\frac{1}{4}$ inches, then $3\frac{1}{4}$ inches again to form double hem. Trim away excess fabric at hem at each lower corner.
9. Apply HeatnBond tape along upper inner edge of bottom hem band. Press to fuse bottom hem.
10. Turn under remaining side edge hems and fuse to complete hems.

11. To form pleats at upper edge of panel, start at inner edge to fold about four pleats across upper edge. Allow each pleat to overlap previous pleat by several inches, making sure pleats are mirror images on panels. Pin pleats; apply masking tape across front and back of fabric to temporarily hold pleats in place. Press.

12. If your window frame is sloped like ours, measure and pin-mark the distance from bottom of drape to the points where it will fold at the top to fit the angle. Connect pin marks with long strip of tape indicating slope line on back and front of each panel.

13. At top back of each panel, apply two loop sections of Velcro brand Fabric Fusion tape, spacing tapes to align with top two hook sections on short rods (some of the excess fabric will be folded over the rod when mounted. If your panels are angled at the top like ours, start about 1 inch above angled pinned lines). Fuse tape in place. Trim away excess fabric to about an inch beyond top tape line and treat raw edges with seam sealant. Remove pins. Press tape sections together to mount drapes.

14. For valance, determine desired finished length (about one-fifth of finished length of overall treatment) and add 12 inches. Determine desired valance width; multiply by 2½ and add 6 inches. Cut fabric to these measurements. If panels need to be joined to achieve desired width, follow manufacturer's instructions to fuse HeatnBond tape to join edges with right sides facing, starting at upper edge, then follow step 4 for hem band instructions.

15. Form 1½-inch-deep double side hems; fuse in place using HeatnBond.

(continued on next page)

For striking contrast, these draperies are edged with a 3½-inch band formed by folding over the reversible fabric to make a double hem the same size as the pattern repeat.

(continued from previous page)

16. To create lower contrasting edge, fold wrong side of fabric toward front to form 3¼-inch double hem; fuse in place using HeatnBond.

17. Start at each side edge to fold pleats across each side of upper edge, meeting in center and making sure pleated valance equals desired finish width. Allow each pleat to overlap previous pleat by several inches, making sure pleats are mirror images on each side. Pin pleats in place; apply masking tape across front and back of fabric to temporarily hold pleats in place. Press.

18. Along top back edge of wrong side of valance, apply two loop sections of Velcro brand Fabric Fusion tape, spacing them to align with hook sections on long rod. (If your valance is angled like ours, temporarily install valance on rods and determine fit of sloped ends. Use pins to mark top edge; remove backing and apply one row of tape so it will align with lowest rows of hook sections on angled rods.) Trim away excess fabric an inch above top section of loop tape and treat raw edges with seam sealant. Remove pins.

19. Press tape together to mount valance.

20. Apply additional Velcro brand Sticky-Back Coins along side edges of valance, if needed.

❧ delicate sheers

SKILL LEVEL: beginner

curtain rod to fit width of upper edge of window

drill

steel tape measure

sheer fabric

scissors

iron

HeatnBond ⅝-inch UltraHold fusible tape

press cloths

brackets

Note: Full widths of fabric were used to make our panels, so no side hems were needed. You can do the same if your fabric selvages are attractive.

1. Install curtain rod below valance rod, placing rod ends just past inner ends of short rods used for panels.

2. Measure desired finished length of sheers from floor to rod; add 13 inches for panel cutting length. Cut as many panels as needed for desired curtain fullness (ours are about four times the window width). If panels need to be joined to achieve desired width, fuse together, right sides facing, with HeatnBond, following manufacturer's instructions. Use press cloths above and below fabric to protect iron.

3. If needed, form 1½-inch-deep double side hems; fuse in place, stopping about 14 inches from lower edge.

4. Form 5-inch-deep double lower hem. Trim away excess fabric within hem at each lower corner.

5. If side hems are needed, turn under remaining side edge hems and fuse to complete those hems.

6. Form 1½-inch-deep double upper hem at upper edge; using HeatnBond, fuse to form upper rod pocket. Complete each panel in the same manner.

7. Slide rod into sheer pockets; mount on brackets.

challenge: Taking the edge off a bay. An angled bay window brought dimension, light and wooded views to this master bedroom at the back of the house, but it also accentuated other hard features in the space, like wide, deep moldings and the picture frame molding behind the bed.

solution: A scalloped window valance and graceful, gathered floor-length tiebacks help soften the angular effect. The curtains are strategically positioned to frame and preserve the view. The fabric's earthy tones echo the woodsy outdoor panorama and complement the room's soothing cream-and-pale-blue palette.

✒ dress panels with self valance

SKILL LEVEL: beginner

curtain rod and mounting hardware

steel tape measure

chalk marking pencil

curtain fabric

scissors

pins

iron

matching thread

sewing machine

4-inch-wide fringed trim

large wood sew-on curtain rings
   (to match rod)

hand-sewing needle

Layering can transform a window treatment from simple to sophisticated, with each element adding interest and personality. Flat-front dress panels with a self-valance are trimmed in rope tassels. An adjustable sand-colored shade offers an extra layer of light control.

1. Mount rod above window.

2. Measure the desired width of the window frame and multiply by 2½ for each panel width. Determine the desired length of each panel and add 7 inches. Cut each of the two long fabric panels to these measurements.

3. For upper self valance, use same cutting width as in Step 2. Measure desired length of valance (it should be about one-fifth the length of the long panel) and add 4 inches. Cut each of the two valances to these measurements.

4. Turn under side edges of each long panel and valance ½ inch, then 3 inches, toward wrong side of fabric; pin and press, then topstitch side hems in place.

5. Turn under ½ inch, then 6 inches, on lower edge of each long panel toward wrong side of fabric; pin and press, then topstitch hems in place. Turn lower edge of each valance under ½ inch, then 3 inches, toward wrong side of fabric; pin and press, then topstitch hems in place.

6. Pin fringed trim to lower edge of each valance, turning trim ends to back. Sew close to upper edge of trim.

7. Pin right side of valance to wrong side of long panel along raw upper edges; stitch with ½-inch seam. Fold valance over to right side.

8. Baste through all layers 3 inches from upper edge.

9. Form box pleats along upper edge, making pleats about 2 to 3 inches deep, spacing them evenly and keeping pattern repeat consistent. Pin in place; press, then stitch again over previous basting line.

10. Sew curtain rings near upper edge of each panel, placing a ring near each end and centered over each pleat. Mount curtain on rod.

challenge: How can one make a sunroom with walls of windows more cozy?

solution: Glass can be cold, especially when it's floor-to-ceiling. A continuous floral valance treats multiple windows as a single unit, softening the glass and framing the view without detracting from it.

challenge: Is there an unfussy way to dress up a casual valance?

solution: A plain valance becomes elegant instantly when trimmed with silky tassels. Gathering a straight valance into swags is another quick way to upgrade an ordinary treatment to a grander one.

✤ striped valance

Fancy fringe brings a finishing flourish to our striped valance and soft sheers. The Velcro-attached-trim technique can also be applied to accent pillows or upholstered furniture to tie the room together.

SKILL LEVEL: beginner

steel tape measure

pencil

4½-inch-wide curtain rod (cut to 2 inches wider than outside width of window frame)

drill

Fast2fuse interfacing (fusible on both sides)

fabric

17-inch-wide roll of HeatnBond UltraHold fusible tape (optional; for heavy or textured fabrics only)

nonstick paper (such as baking parchment)

iron

HeatnBond ⅝-inch-wide UltraHold fusible tape

liquid fray preventer

fabric glue

½-inch-wide flat braid trim

fringe or wood bead trim

Velcro brand Fabric Fusion tape

Velcro brand Sticky-Back tape

1. Measure and mark desired rod placement; install rod at marks.

2. Measure from bracket to bracket along rod for valance width. (Our finished valance measures 13 inches high; adjust height, if desired.)

3. Cut Fast2fuse to measured valance width and height (from Step 2).

4. Add 2 inches to width; double height measurement and add 1 inch. Measure, mark and cut fabric to these measurements (optional: for heavy or textured fabric; also cut HeatnBond sheet to these measurements and, if needed, abut sections of HeatnBond to achieve width). Fuse HeatnBond to wrong side of fabric; trim fabric edges.

5. Cover work surface or ironing board with nonstick paper. Place Fast2fuse on paper; place fabric, right side up, so it overlaps interfacing by 2 inches along one long edge. Fuse interfacing to fabric along this edge. Lift interfacing and fabric; flip over. Smooth fabric over interfacing; fuse front side, making sure to press over paper. Flip again and fuse back, overlapping fabric along starting edge. Fuse strip of HeatnBond tape under overlap; remove backing paper and fuse through all layers.

6. Trim fabric side edges even with interfacing. Apply fray preventer to all raw fabric edges.

7. Glue braid trim to short ends of valance.

8. Apply loop section of Velcro brand Fabric Fusion tape ⅜-inch from upper edge of wrong side of valance. Apply hook section of tape ¼ inch from lower edge of valance on wrong side.

9. Cut a strip of fringe equal to width of valance. Cut loop section of Velcro brand Fabric Fusion tape to same length; fuse to right side of fringe heading. Trim loop strip to fit width of trim's flat edge or lip. Fuse loop strip to right side of fringe lip. Press sections together to attach trim.

10. Apply a strip of hook section of Velcro brand Sticky-Back tape along upper edge of rod and brackets.

11. Position valance on rod, aligning hook and loop sections of tape.

You can change the look of this valance in a snap with our flexible-fringe technique, which allows you to switch out one trim for another in seconds.

❧ soft sheers

SKILL LEVEL: beginner

steel tape measure

curtain rod cut to fit outer width of window frame

drill

sheer fabric

scissors

HeatnBond Lite $5/8$-inch-wide fusible tape; press cloths

iron

1. Measure and mark position of rod above window. Install curtain rod.

2. Measure desired length of sheers from floor to rod; add 13 inches for panel length. Measure rod length; multiply by 2 to obtain panel width. Cut two panels to these measurements. If panels need to be joined to achieve desired width, fuse together, right sides facing, with HeatnBond, following manufacturer's instructions. Use press cloths above and below fabric to protect iron.

3. Place panels right side down. Turn in 1½-inch double hems at side edges; press. Fuse HeatnBond tape along edges of these hems, placing it close to folded edge. Press to hem side edges, stopping about 14 inches from lower edge.

4. Turn up 5-inch double hem at lower edge. Trim away excess fabric within hem at each lower corner.

5. Fuse HeatnBond tape along upper edge of this hem, placing it close to upper folded edge. Press to hem lower edge.

6. Finish fusing side hems.

7. Turn in 1½-inch double hem at upper edge. Fuse in same manner as side hems to form upper rod pocket. Complete each panel in same manner.

8. Slide rod into pockets; mount on brackets.

❧ shaped valances

SKILL LEVEL: beginner

steel tape measure

3- to 6-inch-wide ½-inch-thick
   mounting board

hand saw

yardstick

decorator fabric

scissors

butcher paper

pins

fabric

beaded trim (optional)

sewing machine

matching thread

iron

staple gun

L-shaped metal brackets

½- to ³⁄₄-inch screws

1½-inch screws

drill and ⅛-inch drill bit

---

1. Measure window width from outside of molding. Cut mounting board 4 to 6 inches wider than window width. For valance width, add twice the width of the mounting board plus length of mounting board plus 1 inch for seam allowances.

2. For length of valance, measure height from the bottom of the window frame to the top of the valance. (Note: We mounted the valance 7 inches above the window, a distance that was also added to the total window height). Divide this measurement by 5, add 3 inches for the header, plus ½ inch for the seam allowance.

3. Calculate the amount of fabric needed for each valance by measuring the width of the fabric you have chosen for your project. If the width of the valance is less than the width of the fabric, you will need only one length of fabric for each valance. Otherwise you'll need to piece the fabric to get desired width. If so, be sure to match patterns and center repeat. Cut fabric.

4. To create a shaped edge for the valance, cut a piece of butcher paper the width of the finished valance. For the shaped edge shown, use the template (see page 127) to create a pattern. Adjust the size and shape of the edge to suit the size of your valance (see *How to Enlarge Patterns*, page 127). Fold valance fabric in half, centering repeat. Place and pin pattern on fabric, aligning center edge with fold line and trace the lower edge with a fabric marking pen. Trim along the marked edge. (Note: If you are making more than one valance, line up repeats so each valance looks the same.)

5. Mark and cut matching panels for lining. For self-lined valances, match the fabric repeats just as you did for the valance face. Match the valance to the valance lining, right sides facing. If desired, add piping or trim at this time, sandwiching and pinning trim between valance and lining. Stitch across the lower edge of the valance. Trim and clip seam allowances. Understitch the seam.

6. Fold the seam allowances to the lining side and stitch the side seams together. Turn the valance right side out; press.

7. Measure the length of the valance and adjust to fit. Clean finish the top edge with a wide zigzag stitch, or serge the edge if you have an overlock machine available.

8. Fold and press 3 inches toward back along top edge of valance. Center valance along top edge of mounting board and staple in place, overlapping fabric around corners.

9. Screw brackets into underside of mounting board (with ½- to ³⁄₄-inch screws). Hold valance over window and mark placement of screw holes through brackets onto wall. Screw in place (with 1½-inch screws). Repeat Steps 4 through 9 for each valance.

floral valance

Make a stylish statement with this pretty shaped valance. The lined flat panel features a gently scalloped bottom edge that gives it grace and piping all around to give it polish. It is simple to make, and even easier to install—the clip-on curtain rings eliminate the need for a rod casing. For a super, no-sew alternative, substitute a table runner embellished with fringe or ribbon trim.

SKILL LEVEL: beginner

steel tape measure
metal ruler
kraft paper
pencil
scissors
pins
decorator fabric
piping cord
matching thread
sewing machine with zipper foot
iron
hand-sewing needle

1. Measure width of outside window frame and determine depth of valance from top to lowest point along bottom hem. Add 1 inch to both measurements and draw a rectangle to these dimensions on kraft paper. Cut out. Fold paper in half crosswise (short ends together). To make pattern, draw a gentle curve freehand along bottom edge to shape as desired, and cut along the marked line. Open pattern.

2. Pin pattern to fabric, centering over fabric repeat, and cut one valance piece. Repeat to create one lining piece.

3. Add together measurements of all four sides of valance plus 20 inches for curves and cut a piece of piping to this length.

4. From decorator fabric, cut several 2-inch-wide bias strips of fabric. Square off the ends of strips and sew short ends together with ½-inch seams to form one continuous casing, long enough to cover the piping cord. Wrap casing over piping cord, right side out raw edges matching, and stitch as close to cord as possible using a zipper foot. Trim the raw edges to ½ inch.

5. Pin piping to valance face fabric, right side up raw edges matching. Cut piping cord where ends meet so that they abut neatly, opening casing and cut fabric, leaving ½ inch of fabric to extend past each end of cord. Fold in one end of casing to finish and pin in place. Sew piping to valance using zipper foot. Remove pins.

6. Place lining fabric over face fabric, right sides facing and raw edges matching with piping sandwiched between, and pin in place. Stitch along all sides close to piping, leaving an opening along top edge for turning. Remove pins.

7. Trim seams, turn right side out and press; hand stitch opening closed.

❧ petite valance

NO SEW

SKILL LEVEL: beginner

fusible adhesive

scissors

steel tape measure

fabric

iron

Velcro brand Sticky Back tape

curtain rod: standard; 2½-inch wide,
    flat; 2½-inch wide, flat tension

string

Note: Cut fabric to 3 times
window width plus 6 inches for
1½-inch double-side hems. To
desired height, add 4 inches for
2-inch double bottom hem and
2 inches for the top edge.

1. With fusible adhesive, fuse bottom then side hems.

2. Press in box pleats, turn top edge down and iron pleats in place with loop section of Fabric Fusion tape.

3. Apply hook section of Sticky Back tape across front of rod.

4. Join hook and loop tapes and flip valance over top edge of rod to the front. Install rod with front side of rod next to window.

ALTERNATIVES

unique tassel

Bring a touch of spring to your decor year-round with this pretty, easy-to-make floral shade pull. Snip a few sprigs of faux lily of the valley, gather them into an eye-pleasing arrangement, then position the end of an 8-inch-long ribbon about 1 inch from the ends of one side of the stems.

Stretch the ribbon along the length of the stems, fold it to form a ½-inch loop beyond the stem ends, then stretch it back down along the other side of the stems. Wind the remaining ribbon tightly around the stems and ribbon, up toward the loop and back down again, tucking the end under the wrapped ribbon, trimming if needed. Tie a bow through the loop and hand sew the tassel onto the shade.

sew-easy options

Adding trims or flourishes to ready-made curtains or panels lets you create custom treatments in no time. Consider the following ideas:

➤ **create stylish tiebacks** by cutting 16- or 18-inch-square colored or printed napkins into 4- or 4½-inch-wide strips. Sew two strips together along one short edge, press cut edges over ¼ inch to the front, then stitch braid or grosgrain borders all around over the edges. Stitch on a small, square hook-and-loop tape closure at the free ends of each strip. Then tack on a contrasting button to hide the closure.

➤ **sew fringe or a ball trim** along the inside edges and lower hems of rectangular table linens or sheets (make sure they're long enough to cover your window) and mount on a rod with clip-on curtain rings. The fringe will move gracefully when summer breezes blow through.

➤ **stitch crocheted lace edging** to ready-made sheer panels for Victorian flair. For maximum staying power, be sure to use sturdy cotton thread when sewing this thick lace trim to your window coverings.

trend watch *Fancy tiebacks*

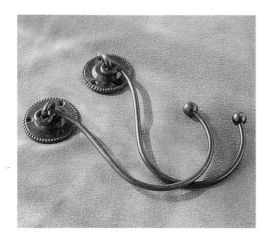

refined: Add a hint of French Country elegance with this hand-painted porcelain.

polished: For a touch of tradition, try these holdbacks with a subtle rim design.

baroque: Romantic backs with an Acanthus design add regal appeal.

playful: Fly high with these fun metal airplane holdbacks.

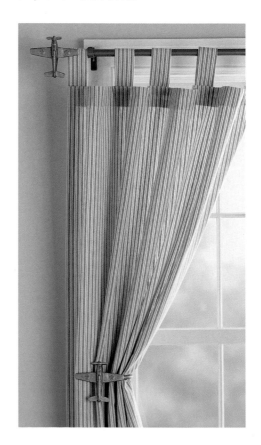

contemporary: For a mod look, opt for metal holdbacks.

eclectic:
Complement your decor with one of these holdbacks in a wide selection of shapes and styles.

Elegant fringe trim combined with four strands of beads creates a chic, colorful tieback that secures this simple drape with a pom-pom flourish.

Fusing style with function, tiebacks are a quick way to add personality to window treatments. With their innovative details, striking colors and unique use of textures, they can gussy up even a plain pair of inexpensive draperies. Here are some tips to create easy, one-of-a-kind tiebacks with style.

❧ **evoke a seaside mood.** Create a casual feel with sailcloth draperies tied back with strands of seashells, boating rope in a decorative knot or craft-store starfish hot-glued to netting.

❧ **raid the jewelry drawer.** Vintage jeweled clip earrings centered on a velvet ribbon create smart tiebacks. Or simply gather draperies with matching strands of costume pearls or beaded necklaces.

❧ **tie on trims.** Cut decorative tassel trim or bullion fringe to create striking tiebacks; sew fabric rings in a matching color to act as hooks. Embroidered ribbons tied in a bow make lively tiebacks for kitchen curtains.

❧ **draw from nature.** Fashion tiebacks out of woven raffia and intersperse with tiny silk flowers and dried leaves. Or add strands of colorful beads for oomph.

❧ **add sparkle.** Sew or glue glistening beads, sequins or buttons to wide satin ribbons. Or tie ribbons into big bows and dangle flea market crystals from old chandeliers in the center of each tieback.

no-sew simple

Consider these extra no-fuss window ideas:

❧ **add grommets** about 8 inches apart along one end of a blanket or quilt. Thread grosgrain ribbon or sturdy twine through the grommet holes and tie to a rod or pole.

❧ **create a fun, fast valance** by folding cheery dinner napkins in half on the diagonal and draping them over a thick wooden pole with the pointed ends down.

❧ **mount shelves across window** and fill them with colorful glass bottles, seashells or small potted plants.

❧ **wind a silk flower garland** around a pole to create a valance. Drape tendrils at both ends like cascades.

❧ **install a shelf above a window** that can serve as both a pelmet and a display area. Cut curtain wire to fit between the brackets, add hooks inside the brackets, tie on the wire, suspend S-shaped hooks from the wire and hang teacups or small pitchers from the hooks.

❧ **seek out fabrics with open hems,** such as fancy linen hand towels in large sizes, to thread on a tension rod to create instant shades.

50 ways to...
revitalize window treatments

Fashions change. With window treatments, as with outfits, you can achieve a new look with accessories or unusual combinations. Here are ways to revitalize your windows with buttons, bows, trims, tassels and layers of fabric to be right in style.

→ Trim curtains with flirty lace.

→ Add a fabulous button to the side of a drape (a little more than halfway up), sew a loop on the opposite bottom edge and hook the drape back.

→ Use wide lengths of plaid chiffon ribbon in place of roll-up cords to tie up bamboo shades to a desired length.

→ Attach a favorite map to a plain shade with spray adhesive. Replace the shade pull with a souvenir of the country featured (a miniature Eiffel Tower, a pair of Delft shoes) tied on with a piece of twine or ribbon.

→ Give an athlete's room a sporty touch with old varsity letters, baseballs or hockey pucks added to tiebacks.

→ Doll up a nursery window with a clothesline valance. Run cording from one side of the window to the other. Use miniature clothespins to hang dolls' clothes on the line.

→ Recycle Dad's ties to create silken tiebacks for drapes in the study or den. Cut off the width at the bottom of three ties; then braid together the remaining sections, turn under ends and finish off with a hot-glue gun. Use pushpins to attach the tiebacks to either side of the window frame.

→ Drape vintage scarves over old sheers.

→ Paint a decorative frieze above a window that echoes the patterns or designs on the drapery panels.

→ Trim gingham curtains with rickrack.

→ Bedeck a silk swag with beaded trim.

→ Stamp a design on a plain shade.

→ Soften a half-shuttered window with a fabric valance. Screw a series of glass knobs into the window frame. Sew tabs on a long, narrow length of fabric and tie the fabric loosely to the knobs.

→ Paint a trompe-l'oeil outdoor scene on a window shade.

→ Drape a swag of dried flowers or evergreens over a window to create a natural valance.

→ Spray paint a wooden rod in gold.

→ Drape saris over window rods (jeweled knobs make great finials).

→ Replace hooks with silk flowers. Twist stems to fasten curtains to rods.

Add a decorative flair to your window treatments with (top to bottom) a bullion fringe, tassel fringe or beaded trim.

- Give café curtains an hourglass figure. Add a rod at the hem and cinch the middle with a fabric tie.
- Add a wide band of paisley or toile to the top of plain drapes. Flip it over the rod to create a contrasting valance.
- Distinguish simple piqué curtains with interesting appliqués.
- Overlay dark curtains with sheers.
- Topstitch curtains with satin ribbon.
- Sew together a patchwork curtain using squares of various floral curtains.
- Fold a long lace panel over a rod.
- Gather the middle with a tassel.
- Add velvet to the hem of floor-length curtains so they puddle on the floor.
- Spruce up shutters with several coats of paint in fabulous new hues.
- Tack a shawl or gauze panel to the window frame. Let sides drape softly, mimicking a jabot.
- Frame a crocheted doily or lace handkerchief between Plexiglas panels. Glue on a braid border, then hang in a window.
- Use paint and textiles to transform a plain white sheet into a charming curtain. First paint on rectangular shapes; then stencil a leaf or other simple design in the middle of each rectangle. Slip a curtain rod through the hem of the sheet and hang it up to instantly enliven a room.
- Turn a table runner into a valance: attach wooden rings to the long edge and hang it on a rod installed above the existing curtain rod.
- Randomly sew silk flowers onto plain sheer curtains to create a garden-fresh ambience.
- Drape voile that is twice the length of the window over a curtain rod (sew hems or edge with iron-on webbing) and knot it in front for easy, casual chic.
- Add fun patterns to a shade using decorative punches.
- Reinvent the concept of café curtains: Cut a wool blanket to fit the window. Punch grommet holes near the top edge. Thread picture wire through the holes from one side of the window to the other. Twist the wire onto funky knobs; attach to screws in the frame.
- Jazz up a plain bamboo shade with spray-painted stripes.
- Write favorite sayings on plain cotton panels with fabric markers.

- Sew bullion fringe on brocade panels for added elegance.

- To achieve a garden view, transfer color photocopies of favorite flowers to a shade with color transfer gel.

- Craft unique shutters from wooden frames and tin ceiling tiles. Build frames to fit the window niche and glue in tin insets to fill.

- Swag windows in the spring with silk roping, floral garlands and strands of beading. In fall, use silk leaves and autumnal colors; in winter, invest in silver and gold trimmings.

- Set sail with blue canvas curtains. Tie them with nautical roping to boat cleats mounted on the wall.

- Turn a crocheted tablecloth into a romantic window treatment. Hang it on a rod using attractive shower curtain hooks slipped through the holes.

- Build a cornice and cover it with fabric to coordinate with drapes.

- Cut a chain of paper dolls (or stars, animals or fish) from colorful cotton and hang over curtains in a kid's room.

- Install shoji panels in a niche to filter light and add an oriental ambience.

- Use a branch, oar, fishing rod, pool cue or hockey stick as a curtain rod.

- Drape a serape over a rod and scoop it to one side with a giant paper flower.

- Arch a long grapevine around a window and decorate it with a string of white lights.

decorative folding screens and shutters control light and add character, too

Curtains are the obvious option for covering windows, but the hassle of measuring, hanging and, yes, washing them can make you yearn for a more immediate, fuss-free solution. To the rescue come decorative folding screens. Not only are they great for partitioning rooms and hiding equipment, but screens also serve as excellent window enhancements. Depending on how they're constructed, they can block light altogether or diffuse and dapple

it like the leaves of a tree. An ideal substitute for curtains, Romans and other soft treatments, screens mimic the effect of doors, creating an illusion of space beyond the window and giving rooms a more expansive feel. Like screens, folding shutters—whether solid panels adorned with molding or classic louvered ones—offer another option for adding an architectural feel that softer treatments can't deliver.

3

4

5

1 Recessed panels of perforated aluminum create these screen-like shutters that let in plenty of light while masking a less-than-stellar view.

2 Lavishly detailed fretwork screens painted in a soothing hue permit sunlight to enter in wonderful patterns, adding a dreamy quality to this bedroom.

3 Like a miniature version of a screen, hinged shutters with adjustable louvers are the perfect choice for bathrooms, offering both light and complete privacy when needed.

4 Authentic period hinged-panel shutters offer crisp contrast to a soft sheer panel. They can also be posed to shield glare or let in light as desired.

5 With their color-washed limed oak finish, these handsome dining room shutters make a bold statement. Nail heads complement the heavy hinges that allow them to assume many positions.

⋇ glossary

batting: Synthetic or cotton material used for padding cornice boards.

café curtain: A single pair of short panels hung half the length of the window.

cascades: Often called tails or jabots, these are usually crisply pleated and tapered panels that flank both sides of a swag; they can be long or short.

cellular shade: A window shade with honey-combed air spaces that allow light through, but create an insulating effect.

cornice: Decorative molding or a rigid frame mounted outside the window frame as an architectural element. This element can be painted, papered or covered with fabric.

curtain clips and **rings:** Used to hang valances from curtain rods or poles.

eyelet: A small metal or plastic ring to hold a cord.

grommet: Metal ring used to secure a hem and reinforce a hole in curtain fabric for rings or laces.

inside mount: When brackets are mounted inside the window frame or opening rather than on the surrounding wall.

jabot: Vertically folded fabric that cascades down either side of a swag or between two or three swags; a term used interchangeably with cascade or tail.

lambrequin: A cornice, often padded and upholstered, that extends all or part of the way down the sides of a window.

mounting board: A wooden board to which a valance or pelmet is attached and which is then installed either inside or outside the window frame.

outside mount: When brackets are mounted on the wall outside the window frame or opening.

panel: A generic term used to describe any floor-length window treatment. This term is also used to describe cut lengths of fabric.

pelmet: Shaped valance made from fabric stiffened with fusible interfacing (an iron-on material used to make fabric rigid) or self-adhesive pelmet former (an adhesive paper used to stiffen fabric) and

positioned on a mounting board; a British term often interchanged with cornice or valance.

puddling: The elegant effect of panels hemmed to be longer than floor length. The excess fabric is bunched together in a pile on the floor.

return: The portion of the window treatment that extends, at both corners, from the face of the mounting board or rod to the wall.

rod pocket: A method of hanging a window treatment where an actual pocket is stitched at the top to slide a curtain rod through.

roman shade: A fabric shade with strategically placed rings spaced horizontally at equal intervals down its entire length that enable it to be raised and lowered by a pull cord. When raised, the shade gathers into soft folds.

stackback: The amount of wall space needed to accommodate a fully opened drapery.

swag or **festoon:** One or more pieces of fabric draped in a scallop-like shape over a rod or mounted on a shelf. The element normally ends on either side in jabots, cascades, or tails.

swag and **tie-back holders:** Elements used to support draped fabric treatments.

tab top: The flat fabric loops at the top of a panel that a rod slides through.

tail: Pleated or gathered fabric that flanks the sides of a swag. Tails can be attached separately or they can trail over from a single length of fabric draped over a rod. These are also often referred to as jabots or cascades.

valance: A gathered, pleated, shaped, or draped window heading. Often constructed like a short curtain, a valance may be edged with a border or other trim and mounted either inside the window opening or outside the window frame.

valance rails: A single rail (for a valance only) or combination track and rail for curtain and valance.

window scarf: A length of fabric casually draped over or hung from a pole or rod at the top of a window like a valance or swag and tails.

How to Enlarge Patterns

Using a colored pencil and ruler, mark a grid on the pattern by connecting grid lines around the edges. On a sheet of paper, mark a grid of 1-inch squares (or size given), making the same number of squares as on the pattern. To do this, use graph paper with 1-inch squares. In each square, draw the same lines as in the corresponding square on the pattern. Another way to enlarge is by using a photocopier.

Italian Stringing Technique, page 51

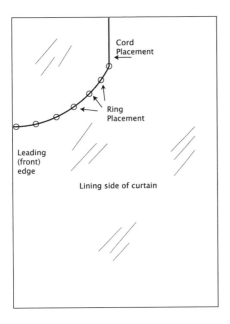

Valance, page 109

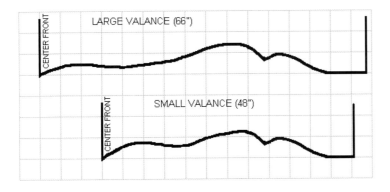

⇝ photo credits

Cover: Designer's Guild; back cover: all rights reserved. page 2: Rob Melnychuk; page 6: Mark Lohman; page 10: Alahambra Hardware; page 11: Stroheim; page 12 top: United Supply Company; page 12 bottom: Helser Brothers; page 13: Susan McWhinney; pages 13, 15, 16 left: Steve Stankiewicz; page 16 right: Anastassios; page 17: Susan McWhinney; page 18: Aimee Herring; page 20: Philip Clayton-Thompson; page 22: Steven Mays; page 23 top: Philip Ennis; page 23 bottom: Mark Lohman; page 24: Jeff McNamara; page 25: Jennifer Lévy; page 27: John Gruen; page 28: Ryan Benyi; page 29: Marcus Tullis; pages 30–31: Dana Huff/Beateworks/Corbis; page 33: Keith Scott Morton; page 34: Tria Giovan; page 36: Liz Glasgow; page 38: Mark Lohman; page 39: Marcus Tullis; page 40: Richard Leo Johnson; page 41: Philip Clayton-Thompson; page 42: Marcus Tullis; page 43: Brian Vanden Brink; pages 44, 45: Mark Lohman; page 46: Ed Gohlich; pages 48, 49 bottom: Smith + Noble; page 49 top: J. Savage Gibson; page 50: Philip Clayton-Thompson; page 52: Mark Samu; page 53: Keith Scott Morton; page 54: Jeff McNamara; page 55 top: Mark Lohman; page 55 bottom: Brad Simmons; pages 56, 57: Steven Mays; page 58: Perfect Glue; page 59: Marcus Tullis; page 60: Steve Vierra; page 61: Philip Clayton-Thompson; page 62: Ryan Benyi; page 63: Aimee Herring; page 64 top: Mark Lohman; page 64 bottom: Philip Ennis; page 65: Brad Simmons; pages 66, 67: Marcus Tullis; page 68 top: Mark Scott/Ideal Home; page 68 bottom: Brian Vanden Brink; page 69: Aimee Herring; page 70: Deborah Ory; page 72: Kate Roth; page 73: Ryan Benyi; page 74: Keith Scott Morton; pages 76–77: Nancy Hill; page 78: Mark Lohman; pages 79, 80: Eric Roth; pages 82–83: Tim Street-Porter; page 84: Designer's Guild; page 86: Keith Scott Morton; page 87: Mark Lohman; page 89: Deborah Ory; pages 90, 91, 95: Keith Scott Morton; page 92: Nancy Hill; pages 96, 97: Smith + Noble; page 99: Deborah Ory; page 101: Rob Melnychuk; pages 102–103: Eric Roth; page 104: Keith Scott Morton; page 105 top: Jessie Walker; page 105 bottom: Brian Vanden Brink; pages 106, 107: Deborah Ory; page 108: John Gruen; page 110: Marcus Tullis; page 111: Ryan Benyi; page 112: Edmund Barr; page 114: Aimee Herring; pages 116, 117: all rights reserved; page 118: Kit Latham; page 120: J.C. Penney; page 121: all rights reserved; pages 124, 125: Glidden.

UFF DA!

By **C. L. G. Martin**

Illustrations by **Richard Clark**

TRICYCLE PRESS
Berkeley/Toronto

To my family—Jerry, Tony and Jessica,
and Erika, Darren, and Tyler.

C. L. G. M.

SCANDINAVIAN TERMS USED IN THIS BOOK:

Lefse (LEF suh): A round soft flat bread made primarily of potatoes. It is served with a meal or spread with butter, sprinkled with sugar and cinnamon, and rolled into a log for a snack.

Lutefisk (LOO tuh FIHSK): Unsalted dried cod prepared in the traditional Norwegian way. Scandinavian Americans often serve lutefisk on Christmas or New Year's Eve.

Uff da! (UF dah): Scandinavian expression used to indicate dismay or concern. Roughly equivalent to "Good grief!"

TRICYCLE PRESS
a little division of Ten Speed Press
P.O. Box 7123
Berkeley, California 94707
www.tenspeed.com

Design by Susan Van Horn
Typeset in Chaparral and Fink Gothic
The illustrations in this book were rendered in mixed media.

Library of Congress Cataloging-in-Publication Data
Martin, C. L. G.
Uff da! / by C. L. G. Martin ; illustrations by Richard Clark.
p. cm.
Summary: Timmer finally finds a way to help his extended Scandinavian
American family when they gather to help fix up an old house.
ISBN 1-58246-117-1
1. Scandinavian Americans--Juvenile fiction. [1. Scandinavian
Americans--Fiction. 2. Family life--Fiction. 3. Dwellings--Fiction.] I.
Clark, Richard, 1969- ill. II. Title.
PZ7.M356776 Uf 2004
[E]--dc22
2003013837

First Tricycle Press printing, 2004
Printed in Singapore

1 2 3 4 5 6 — 08 07 06 05 04

"**What a dump!**" said Melody Margaret.

"It's a real fixer-upper," said Dad.

"Some curtains, a little paint,
it'll be fine," said Mother.

"**Uff da!**" said Grampie Gustie
with a shake of his head.

"I'll help!" said Timmer.

Timmer peeked into room after room. "There's **no glass** in the **windows**!" he yelled.

"**Uff da!** Timmer, bring to me the phone!" shouted Grampie Gustie.

"Hallo? T'ird Cousin T'urston? We need you to make for us your best-in-the-world stained glass windows. You come. Ya?"

"The rugs are **full** of **moth holes!**" Timmer called from the hallway.

"**Uff da!** Timmer, bring to me the phone!" shouted Grampie Gustie. "Hallo? Great Gramma Gerta? We need you to braid for us your best-in-the-world rag rugs. You come. Ya?"

By morning Great Gramma Gerta was settled in and ripping everything that wasn't tied down into rags for her rugs.

"Can I help braid?" asked Timmer.

"Little fingers **aren't** for braiding," she said.

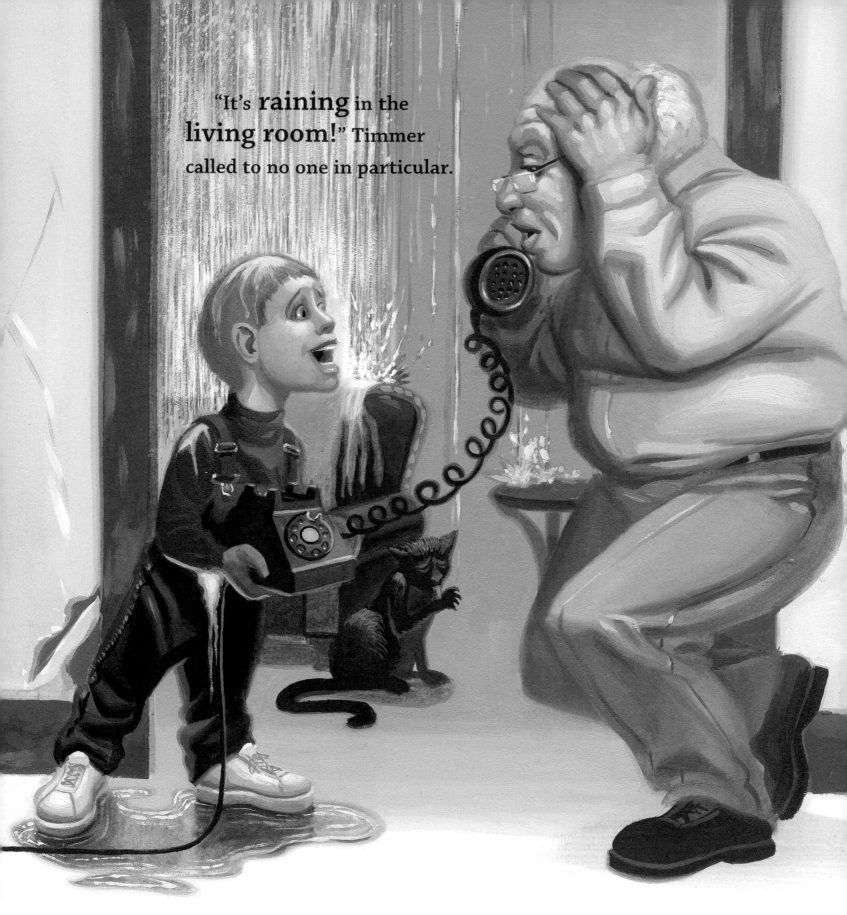

"It's **raining** in the **living room!**" Timmer called to no one in particular.

"**Uff da!** Timmer, bring to me the phone!" shouted Grampie Gustie. "Hallo? Uncle Balancing Butch and the Balancing Bergenborgstroms? We need you to do for us your best-in-the-world balancing and fix our leaky roof. You come. Ya?"

The Balancing Bergenborgstroms moved in the next day.

Timmer shaded his eyes. "Can I help patch the roof?" he asked eagerly.

"**You?!**"

The Balancing Bergenborgstroms laughed.

Swish-swish went Dad's paintbrush and **rrrrrrrrr** hummed Mother's sewing machine.

"Can I help?" Timmer hollered.

"Painting and sewing take lots of practice, Dumpling," Mother said.

"The **basement's** full of **water!**" he yelled over his shoulder.

"**Uff da!** Timmer, bring to me the phone!" shouted Grampie Gustie.

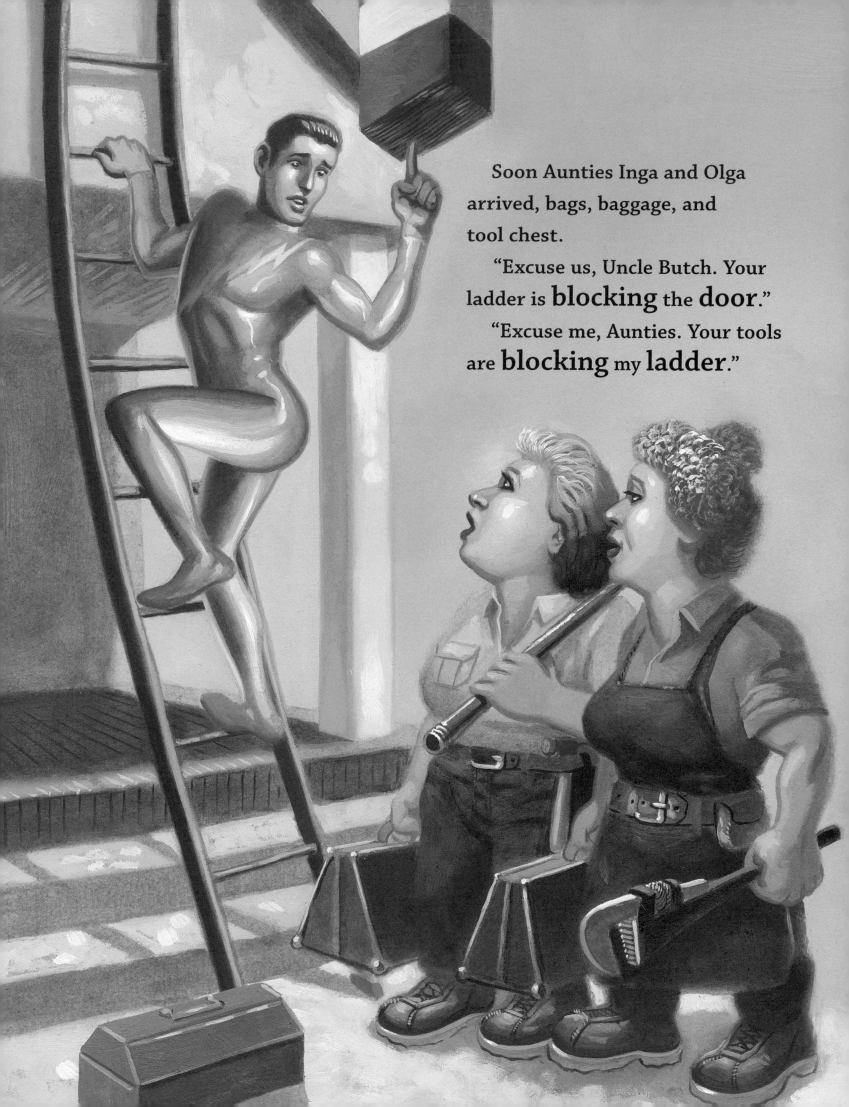

Soon Aunties Inga and Olga arrived, bags, baggage, and tool chest.

"Excuse us, Uncle Butch. Your ladder is **blocking** the **door**."

"Excuse me, Aunties. Your tools are **blocking** my **ladder**."

In no time they ripped out every cracked, crusty pipe in the house.

"I know how to use a wrench," Timmer said.

"Plumbers need **big** muscles," Aunties Inga and Olga said together.

While the house **banged** and **clanged**, Timmer collected everyone's scraps and built his own little town.

At dinnertime Timmer squeezed unnoticed into his chair. Hungry arms grabbed for food and all he got was a pickled herring and a piece of *lefse*.

"Isn't this cozy?"
said Mother.

"We could use help with **all** this **cooking!**" Melody Margaret said.

By sunrise, Great Grandpap Sea Dog Sven was cooking breakfast. "Are you one of my great grandchildren?" he asked Timmer.

"I guess so. Can I flip the meat cakes?"

"The galley's no place for little sailors," barked Sea Dog Sven. "Sharp knives, hot pans, spitting grease! **Watch out, Matey!**"

Timmer trudged to his room. He made Timmertown **bigger**.
Whatever Timmertown needed Timmer made all by himself.

Outside Timmer's room the house was not as orderly.

"**Hurry up** in that bathroom!" called a crabby voice.

"**Wait your turn!**" growled another.

"Hey, someone **ripped up** my favorite **shirt!**"

"That old thing? It makes a **better rag** than a shirt, **dearie!**"

"Soup's on, Mateys!"
Great Grandpap shouted. The house
rumbled as hungry Bergenborgstroms
raced to dinner.

Slap-flap, slap-flap came Third Cousin Thurston's rubber apron. Stomp-stomp came Grampie Gustie's heavy boots. Clink-clank-clunk came Auntie Inga's and Auntie Olga's tool belts. Closer and closer. Faster and faster. Clickety-clack came Great Gramma Gerta's wheels right over Melody Margaret's toes.

"Yeooooooooouch!" she screeched.

"You **pushed** me!"
"I **tripped!**"

"Ladies **first!**"
"**Sez who?**"

"**Hey,** I didn't get any dumplings,"
Bax complained.

"Well, dear, you have enough *lutefisk* for
three people," said Great Gramma Gerta.

"Are you saying my boy eats **too
much?**" demanded Balancing Butch.

"Not if he were a **brontosaurus**," snapped Grampie Gustie.
"**What?**" shouted Balancing Butch, slamming his fist on the table.

With a splintery **c-c-c-c-c-crack** the table fell into everyone's laps.

"**Uff da!**" cried the whole entire Bergenborgstrom family and they stomped away in every direction.

"I'll get some glue!" Timmer said.

No one answered.

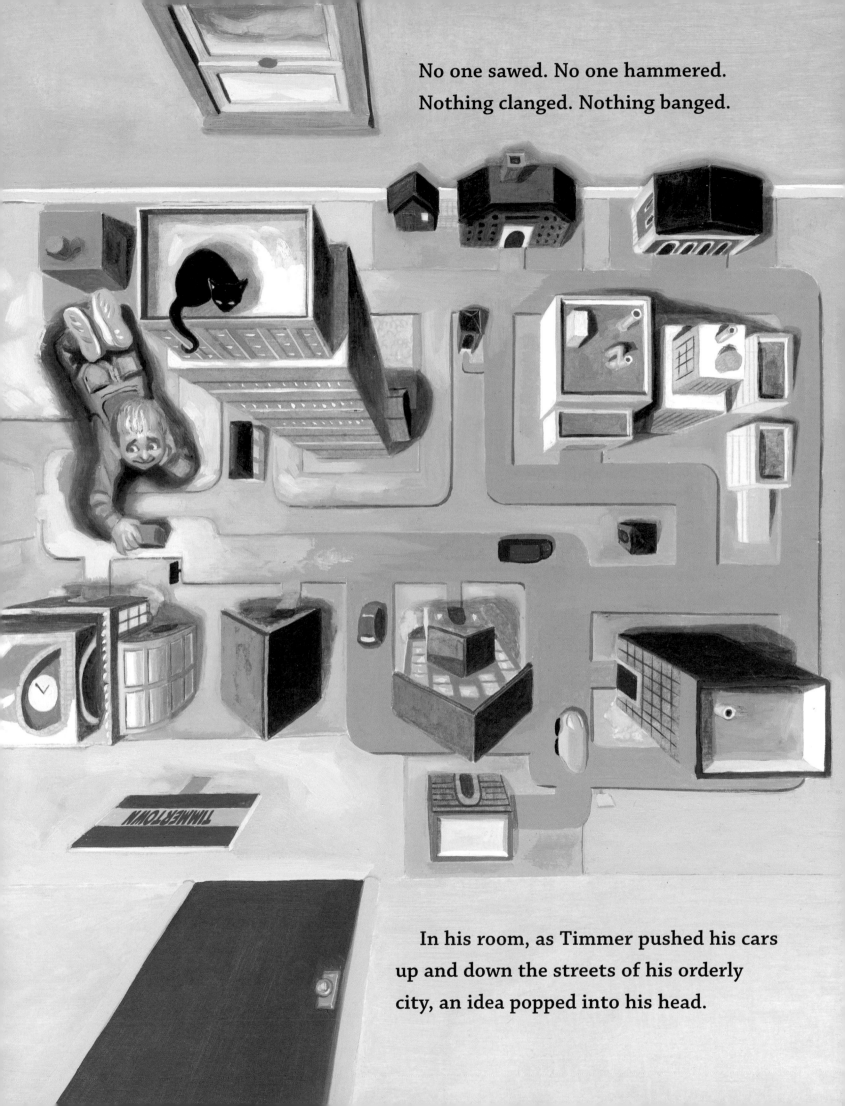

No one sawed. No one hammered.
Nothing clanged. Nothing banged.

In his room, as Timmer pushed his cars
up and down the streets of his orderly
city, an idea popped into his head.

"**Soup's on, Mateys!**" Great Grandpap shouted the following morning and all over the house doors creaked open.

"What's this?!" grumbled a chorus of crabby voices.

One way came Balancing Butch, Bjorn, Bax, Bea, and Birdie Blythe.

Slow rolled Great Gramma Gerta's wheels.

Aunties Inga and Olga paused to **yield**,

and Mother, Dad, and Melody Margaret marched
single file to **keep right**.

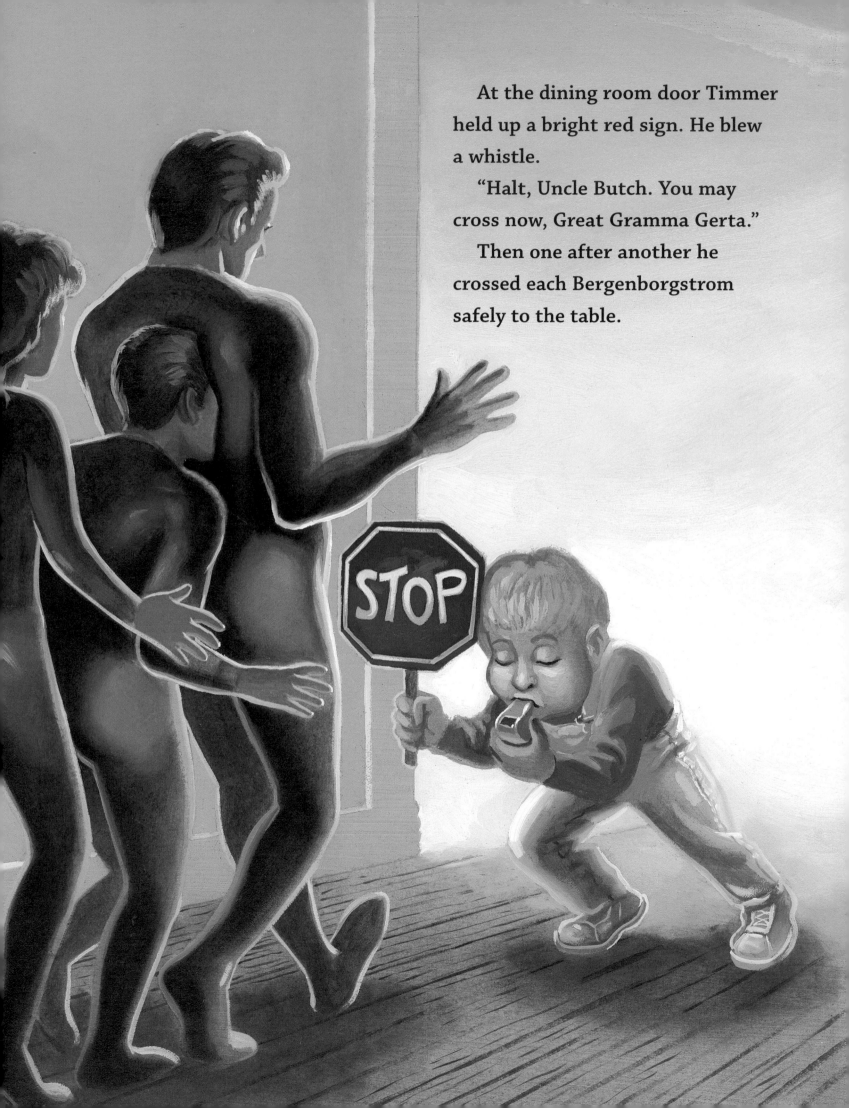

At the dining room door Timmer held up a bright red sign. He blew a whistle.

"Halt, Uncle Butch. You may cross now, Great Gramma Gerta."

Then one after another he crossed each Bergenborgstrom safely to the table.

"Who **hangs** without asking all this **signery?**" Grampie
Gustie bellowed.

Timmer gulped. "M-m-me, Sir."

"Grandson Timmer, from now on you will do for us your
best-in-the-world traffic directoring. You will. Ya?"

Before Timmer could answer, Melody Margaret shrieked, "**Eeeeeek!** Outside! Gophers! **Millions of them!**"

"Grandson Timmer, **bring to me the phone!**" shouted Grampie Gustie.

"Uff da!" cried Timmer.

There were more Bergenborgstroms on the way but there was no need to worry.

The best-in-the-world director of Bergenborgstrom traffic was on the job!